THE SPIRIT AND PASSION
BEHIND THE
PASADENA TOURNAMENT *of* ROSES

MICHAEL K. RIFFEY
WITH LAURA A. ADAMS

STEPHENS PRESS
LAS VEGAS, NEVADA

STEPHENS PRESS • LAS VEGAS, NEVADA

Carolyn Hayes Uber, Publisher
Don and Joan Clucas, Editors
Jim Burns, Managing Editor
Sue Campbell, Creative Director
Chris Wheeler, Art Director

Cataloging in Publication Data Available

ISBN-10: 1-932173-44-7
ISBN-13: 978-1932173-444

STEPHENS
PRESS, LLC
A Stephens Media Company

Post Office Box 1600
Las Vegas, Nevada 89125-1600

Printed in Hong Kong

1500. The Herald. Tournament of Roses

To my lovely wife Anne, my son Todd, and my daughter Elizabeth, who allowed me countless hours away from our family for thirty-nine years having fun with the best volunteers in the world. And to all of my friends in the Tournament of Roses who have the pride and the passion to give back to their community by creating the greatest Parade in the world and the "granddaddy of them all," the Rose Bowl.

PASADENA, Jan. 1st 1896.

WAITE PHOTO

Contents

Preface

It was 1889, and people in New York were buried in snow. Professor Charles F. Holder, president of Pasadena's Valley Hunt Club, looked across the table at his fellows and proposed, "Here our flowers are blooming and our oranges are about to bear. Let's hold a festival to tell the world about our paradise." The club members were themselves former residents of the East and Midwest. They knew about winter, and they knew about marketing. Thus was born a plan to advertise Pasadena's advantages by gathering flowers from local gardens and displaying them as evidence of the delightful Southern California climate.

The following New Year's Day, over 2,000 people viewed a Parade of flower-covered carriages. They also cheered for their favorites among the participants in a tournament of foot races, polo matches, and tugs-of-war held on a town lot that we now call Tournament Park.

Today, millions of viewers around the world continue to celebrate New Year's morning with family and friends by gathering in front of televisions for two hours in "paradise." The carriages draped with flowers have given way to huge, animated floats, each one bedecked with more flowers than the average florist's shop will use in five years. More than fifty musical groups compete annually for the seventeen marching band slots in the Parade, and precision equestrian groups sporting silver trappings dance gracefully along the Parade route on specially treated shoes. Each entrant strives for absolute perfection. This phenomenal collective work of fragrant, living art is created by an army of volunteers and managed by a cadre of 935 members who together annually donate more than 80,000 volunteer hours of personal time. It is led each year by one person privileged to wear a red jacket that identifies him or her as the Tournament's president. The original tournament of races and games and jousting at rings has given way to a football game held in a huge bowl of a stadium, where players from the East vie with players from the West in the post-season game of all post-season games, the Rose Bowl.

I have a white suit. It has been my privilege to be a member of the Tournament of Roses for over thirty-seven years. The experience has humbled me and taught me the beauty of the human spirit.

In addition, a red jacket hangs in my closet beside my white suit. It is now my privilege to wear that jacket on New Year's Day each year. It distinguishes me as the 2004 President of the Pasadena Tournament of Roses, a year that took me and my beautiful wife Anne to a multitude of new places and left us with a wealth of new friends and priceless memories. That year led up to a day that was, for us, beyond perfection.

Oh, sure, some things go wrong in every Tournament, and I plan to tell you about a few of those. But what overwhelms me almost to the point of tears on each beautiful New Year's Day is the spirit, the absolute commitment to excellence in every one of the people involved. The Rose Parade is, as Art Linkletter put it so aptly, "more than a Parade." It is a symbol, a gesture, and a gift from people who have worked hard to create it. And the Rose Bowl game is, of course, "THE GRANDADDY OF THEM ALL."

As the proud representative of 935 of the finest volunteers in the world, it is my profound honor to share with you these stories about the passion, the humor, the sacrifices, the brilliance, and even some sorrows behind the scenes of the Pasadena Tournament of Roses.

Mike Riffey

Foreword

For as long as humankind can remember, we have been awed and captivated by Mother Earth's annual renewal of herself. We observe this miracle across the globe at many of times of the year. We celebrate it on January 1, the first day of the Julian or Roman calendar. The ancient Chinese observed it in late January or early February, the early Celts marked it at summer's end, and, Egyptians of old at the close of September. Despite this variety, however, the purpose for all these observations has always been the same. The human family has forever felt compelled to celebrate and give thanks for the timeless promise of each new year.

The festivities associated with this natural wonder have always been dazzling in their variation and color. Prayers and blessings are given, bells are rung, lanterns lit, debts sometimes forgiven, and we make New Year's resolutions to rejuvenate and rededicate our lives. We've even been known to have Parades and football games!

I believe it can be said that our country's greatest contribution to all of this history has been the creation of the Tournament of Roses. We celebrate here in Pasadena, California, with a uniquely beautiful Parade and traditional football game. The music, the pageantry, and the famous florally decorated floats bring forth each year a dazzling display of creativity, that with the advent of television, have combined to make the Tournament of Roses the world's celebration.

Sometime during the summer of 2003 I received a call from Mike Riffey, a well-known Pasadenan, who introduced himself explaining that he was serving as the President of the 2004 Tournament of Roses. Mike asked if he and his wife Anne could visit me at my workrooms at DreamWorks Studios, and I of course said yes. I at once assumed that Mike wanted me to participate in some musical way at the ceremonies, and I felt happy for the opportunity to meet him. When, during his visit, he explained that he wished me to serve as Grand Marshal of the Rose Parade itself, I was overwhelmed. Glancing at the list of people who have served as Grand Marshal reads like a Who's Who of some of the most distinguished individuals of our time, including Presidents and dignitaries of all kinds. To have been asked to join this list conferred a great honor on me, and although I didn't feel very "grand" or "marshal-like," I did feel tempted to accept.

I couldn't help wondering, however, why Mike wanted me, when we were so close to Hollywood, always bursting at the seams with lustrous celebrities, any one of whom would seize the opportunity with pride, joy, and alacrity. He then explained that his theme for the 2004 Rose Parade was to be music itself, using the words "Music, Music, Music" as his banner slogan for the entire event, and that he wanted a composer to head the Parade. Hearing this, I felt more

comfortable, and although I didn't land in Mike or Anne's lap, I did jump at the chance!

After months of preparation by Mike, Anne, and their volunteers and staff, the great day arrived. Teams of horses were lined up, bands assembled, costumed participants of all kinds gathered, and the great floats were rolled in place to begin the Parade. For two delightful hours, my wife Samantha and I as Grand Marshal and spouse had the privilege of riding in a beautifully restored 1940 Packard Darrin automobile, and we were greeted by an estimated crowd of one million very happy and welcoming people. I particularly remember rounding a corner and seeing a young man seated in the middle of the stands holding up a sign that read, "Samantha rocks!" We felt right at home.

Around the next turn some unexpected fun awaited us. The weather was a little chilly and I had been wearing my Boston Red Sox baseball cap. As we approached a new group of cheering Parade watchers, I noticed a handsome and well-dressed woman wearing a New York Yankees hat. At that time, the red hot competition between the Boston Red Sox and the New York Yankees was at its most heated and prompted me to point to my Red Sox cap as we passed the New York fan. In return, she pointed to her New York Yankees hat and turned around and teasingly mooned me! I think by now most readers will be familiar with this use of the word "moon." This little scene elicited a truly spontaneous and good-natured laugh from the crowd. It seems the warm spirit of the Tournament of Roses transcends even baseball rivalries.

This particular Parade was certainly unique and very special for me. With music as its overarching theme, it attracted young musicians from all over the country in greater numbers than ever before. As a former member of my own high school band, I felt a genuine kinship with all of them and took great pride in being able to represent them as their grand marshal in an army where the real heroes and medal-winners are the parents and teachers.

Probably the most memorable moment in this entire experience came after we arrived at the Rose Bowl to begin the opening ceremonies. All of my life I've conducted orchestras in recording studios,

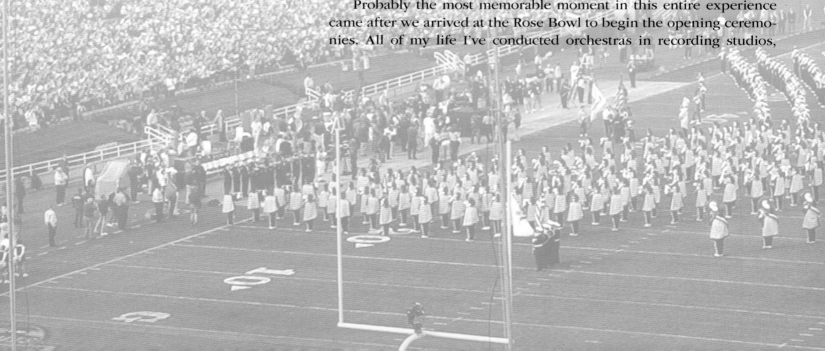

concert halls, arenas, and outdoor venues, but nothing in my experience can compare with being at the base of the beautiful San Gabriel Mountains standing before a crowd of 93,849 excited fans and conducting the combined bands of the University of Michigan and the University of Southern California. I had written a special arrangement of the *Star Spangled Banner* for the occasion and wondered how, with musicians spread out all over the field, we would be able to play together. I worried about things like wind direction and the Doppler effect, but the respective bands had had plenty of playing field experience and not only stayed together, but played brilliantly. After Air Force jets flew overhead and parachutists landed on the field, I then had the privilege of tossing the coin for the opposing football captains to choose sides and begin a fabulous football game which was won by everyone present and watching.

For 115 years, the Tournament of Roses has given us American pageantry at its best. It has become the defining way in which we welcome in the New Year, and to have joined the list of past grand marshals has been a very special honor. I can also double my debt to Mike Riffey for his creation of this splendid book, which is clearly the work of a man who deeply loves the Tournament of Roses and wishes to share its color and extensive history with all of us.

Admittedly, as grand marshal, I have been given the "best seat in the house," and so I can excitedly suggest that if you can be in Pasadena on New Year's Day you will be greatly rewarded. If, however, you're not able to join the festivities in person, this handsomely produced volume will be the next best thing to being there. Enjoy . . . and here's to the next 115 Happy New Years!

John Williams

CHAPTER 1
Happy New Year!

TV interviews get underway before the sun comes up on New Year's morning. Inset, parade goers save their precious spots on the parade route by sleeping on

Happy New Year!

At half-past three o'clock in the morning on New Year's Day, the floats are lined up in silence along Orange Grove Boulevard in Pasadena, California, guarded by police officers and men and women who wear white suits.

The Rose Queen and her Princesses are waking up and taking their showers, ready to be transported to the Tournament House, where hairdressers and makeup artists are assembling to prepare them for their royal ride down Colorado Boulevard.

A fleet of white Honda vans with the Tournament Rose emblazoned on their sides is heading for appointed assignments.

The President of the Tournament of Roses and his or her family are throwing back their bedcovers after a very brief sleep, having stayed up until the early hours of the morning while the floats have submitted to the final judging.

Stephanie Edwards is up and getting dressed in "layers," so that she will be comfortable as the temperature fluctuates throughout the day. She is scheduled to meet Bob Eubanks at the KTLA studio by 4:30 a.m.

The judges, having determined which floats will be heralded with prize banners during the parade, have been escorted to their hotels for a few hours of well-deserved rest.

Teams of reporters and commentators are arising and stretching and heading for the Tournament House, headquarters of the Pasadena Tournament of Roses Association, ready to interview the Grand Marshal and other important dignitaries.

NEVER ON SUNDAY

The Tournament of Roses is never held on Sunday. This was a conscious decision on the part of the Valley Hunt Club members who originated the event. They wanted to avoid alarming the horses tethered in front of the churches along Colorado Boulevard during Sunday morning services. To this day, the Tournament takes place on January 2 every seventh year.

Camera operators are testing equipment and checking timelines.

Beautiful horses, which have been stabled at the Los Angeles Equestrian Center in Burbank, are now receiving their pre-parade grooming and adornments in the area commonly known as "the Pit."

Yawning teenagers are waking up and taking their showers and taming their hairstyles firmly, in preparation for donning their spotless band and drill team uniforms.

Outside, along the five and one-half mile parade route, thousands of people sleep fitfully in sleeping bags on cots and pads and air mattresses, holding the sidewalk spots they have selected for viewing the parade.

Great grandstands wait in the chilly darkness along the route, ready for the folks who have purchased their 24 inches of seating space for the morning.

The VIP stand on Orange Grove Boulevard is already brightly lit in anticipation of the pre-parade show that will take place there just before the Parade begins.

Nine hundred thirty-five white-suited volunteers are moving cheerfully about, manning street barriers that protect the crowds from vehicular interference, making sure that muddy spots below the stand areas are covered with wood shavings, checking identification for all who enter restricted areas, and performing 1,001 other duties that will ensure that the Tournament runs perfectly.

Pasadena Tournament of Roses parade horses have never been bothered by church bells.

Scouts perform a dawn flag ceremony at the Tournament House and the big day gets underway.

The parade will start at 8:01:30 a.m., Pacific Standard Time, and there is much to be done between now and then.

Most Americans, even those on the East Coast, are still sound asleep after celebrating into the wee, small hours of the morning, toasting the arrival of a new year and resolving to make this one better than last. They will wake in a few hours, brew steaming pots of coffee or hot chocolate, and turn to their televisions, where review footage of Times Square's descending ball and *Auld Lang Syne* is about to be replaced by live coverage of marching bands, equestrian units, and the applause that greets each beautiful float. They will watch a show that is viewed by more people around the world than any other. The show will take two hours and ten minutes, and it will appear to run effortlessly. The floats will be lovely and the horses will prance and the bands will stride proudly, and the television commentators will try to convey to the viewers the incredible details of float construction and the interesting facts about each parade entry. It is a wonderful tradition, more than a century.

Throughout my years of Tournament involvement, I have often heard people ask questions about what goes on behind the scenes of the Tournament:

"How do those old cars handle the slow speed for the entire parade?"

"What happens if someone on a float needs to use the restroom?"

"When do the floatbuilders begin their work?"

"How do they make sure that all of those thousands of volunteers know where to glue the flowers on the floats?"

"Who decides what bands get to march in the parade?"

"How does someone get to be the Rose Queen?"

I decided that someone ought to write a book that answered some of those questions, if only for prospective White Suiters in Pasadena. When I mentioned some of my stories to Jim Burns, President of Uber Advertising in Upland, he told me about Stephens Press and convinced me that parade-watchers worldwide might be interested in the workings of the huge event. He and my colleague, Nancy Sinclair, introduced me to Carolyn Uber, Chris Wheeler, and Laura Adams, and all of us went to work. Now you have joined us, reading this book and thereby becoming part of the Tournament family. I hope that you will enjoy learning about the spirit and passion behind, during, underneath, and around all of the pageantry.

Welcome to Pasadena, my friend! And Happy New Year!

A battalion of red and white scooters stand ready for a white-suited army of volunteers.

White suiters help arriving parade goers find their way.

Whether they've come to support a cause; see magnificant floats; cheer their team; have an exhaustingly good time; rub shoulders with royalty, or just to smell the roses all will be more than satisfied at the Pasadena Tournament of Roses Parade.

CHAPTER 2

The Presidency

The Presidency

ight years before I took office, I knew that I would be President of the Pasadena Tournament of Roses in 2004. I had spent 17 years doing committee work and had served as Chairperson on five different committees for two years each. I was appointed as a Director in 1987 and to the Executive Committee in 1996. That year, for the first time, I was given a ticket to view the Parade from the stands. There we were, all Executive Committee members with white suits, sitting in a row. It wasn't an easy experience for my colleagues, for I found it difficult to sit still. I was, and still am, at heart a "street person." I'm always wanting to get up and go help fix things.

The Executive Committee assignment progressed to the oversight of four to five different committees each year thereafter, so that by the time I became President I had firsthand knowledge about all 32 committees. Once a member becomes a Director, he or she can only serve as a Director for 10 years or until age 65, whichever comes first. There are approximately 50 Directors of the Tournament of Roses, including 14 Executive members, 17 chairpersons, and all Past Presidents. A candidate who has proven capable of leadership serves on the Executive Committee for four years as a Vice President, then successively becomes Secretary, Treasurer, Executive Vice President, and finally President. The year following one's Presidency, he or she becomes the Immediate Past President. All Past Presidents automatically become Life Directors.

The 2004 Parade was my first as a Tournament of Roses member. My experience is short, but I can describe it thoroughly in only a few words:
Long,
Tiring,
Wet,
Cold,
And one of the most REWARDING experiences of my life!
I can't wait for next year.
—Kathryn Lillo
Cal Poly Alumna

PASADENA TOURNAMENT OF ROSES FIRST WOMAN PRESIDENT—2006

Libby Evans Wright, 2006 President of the Tournament of Roses, is the first woman to hold that office. Catherine Wright (no relation) was the first woman to pilot a float in the Rose Parade. She drove Eagle Rock's entry in 1916. In 1971 Kathy Howie and Kathy Parker, two nineteen-year-old coeds, were the first women to pilot a float while concealed in the driver's compartment underneath it.

The 2006 President of the Tournament of Roses, Libby Evans Wright, is the very first woman to hold that office. Now retired, she joined the Tournament Association in 1978 when she was living in San Marino and working in Los Angeles. In the 1970s and '80s she served as Vice President and District Regional Manager for Security Pacific Bank. She also served as Senior Vice President of Strategic Management and Planning for two hospitals. She was serving on the Board of a hospital in Arcadia, and the CEO suggested that she join the Tournament. She didn't know much about the Tournament, but wanted to be more involved in the community, so she signed up. Her first assignment was with Public Relations, volunteering as a docent at the Tournament House on Thursdays from 2:00 to 4:00 p.m. to conduct tours. She spent New Year's morning 1979 managing the activities of the pre-parade photographers. As she puts it, she didn't "go to the street" for three years.

Libby did not join the Association with an aspiration to become President of the Tournament of Roses. She just wanted to be part of the whole effort, and was willing to work hard. In the early 1990s she was appointed to a chairmanship. She started as Chair of the TV and Radio Committee. From that position she became a Director, and then moved directly to the Executive Committee. She recalls her shock when Gary Dorn called her, ostensibly to discuss a helicopter problem, and then asked if she would like to join the Executive Committee and be the President in 2006.

After joining the Executive Committee, Libby decided to retire from banking. "My husband Bill told me, 'Give it up! You have enough to do!'" she says with a wry smile. "He is a retired Tournament member, and he knows how important the work is to me. He is my best supporter and my greatest fan, a tremendous asset."

"A lot of people ask how I feel about being the first female President in 117 years of Tournament history. Actually, I don't think of being the first woman; I think of the honor of being the President. I feel that it is a privilege and an honor to be one of 934 candidates, and an even greater honor to be the one selected.

"Our approach," she states calmly, "is not about who made a mistake or who caused a problem. It's about 'How do we fix this?' Every Tournament member is an over-achiever. Having them all in one room at a meeting is fantastic! They know that the experience they're creating makes all of the hard work worthwhile."

One of the most enjoyable assignments for Libby was serving as chair of the Tournament Entries Committee. Her job in that capacity was making sure that the Grand Marshal had a suitable car, got into the car on time, etc. Well, the Grand Marshal happened to be Kermit the Frog, and he was a problem because his handler had to be completely hidden from view; no child could be disappointed to learn that Kermit wasn't real! So, Libby was the person who talked to Roy Adcock about redesigning his beautiful antique car. Fortunately,

RAIN WASN'T IN THE JOB DESCRIPTION.

Parade day 1995, opened chilly, blue, and bright, just as it has for so many charmed years, but the next morning at Post Parade was dark, gray, and threatening. Then in the fourth of my fourteen years with the Tournament, I outfitted myself with proper transparent rain gear over my fresh White Suit and headed out to my float in the light mist.

By mid-morning the light mist had become a persistent drizzle. Lunchtime came and went with no letup, and by mid-afternoon the drizzle had become a steady, beating rain. By the end of the day it was as if I had forgotten my rain gear, I was so wet. My shirt was drenched and turning pink from the bleed off my red tie. When eventually my pants dried, the seams puckered as if sewn by a drunken tailor. (I had them re-sewn by a sober one, and wear them still.)

A miserable day? No, not even close! For I was not out there alone. I was inspired by the thousands who came in spite of the rain to love and admire my float, and to ask me what kind of seeds are these, and what kind of flowers are those? What I discovered that day in the rain was a defining experience: I knew exactly that I was there to serve that love and admiration. I was cold and wet and tired, but loving every minute of it — and I was sorry when it was over. That day in the rain had clearly shown me why I give my time and energy to volunteer for the Tournament of Roses. Every year when I put on my re-sewn white trousers, I am reminded. And every year, I make a point of sharing this story with at least one first-year White Suiter.

—Bob Randall

Roy is a very understanding fellow, and he brought his 1948 Lincoln Continental Cabriolet in to Hollywood on a flatbed truck, installed a convertible top, and equipped the rear end with sound and video. A week before the parade, Roy brought the car to the decorating tent. Curtains were placed around the car so that people couldn't see Allan, Kermit's handler, getting in or out of the car.

It was also Libby's job to walk next to the Grand Marshal's car as it left the Tournament House and headed for the street and the parade. Libby was aghast when a crush of spectators flocked toward her and Kermit! Fearing for their mutual safety, she quickly called in the Sheriff's Mounted Police to handle crowd control. She had never witnessed such a passionate reaction to a Grand Marshal — "They were screaming and hollering! I grabbed my radio and yelled, 'Back up!' I was screaming, but no one seemed to hear. 'Back up!' I yelled again, to no avail. But then, seemingly from his perch on the convertible top, Kermit himself bellowed, 'BACK UP!' That finally did the trick."

At the Rose Bowl, as they were getting ready to drive onto the field, Kermit sang the National Anthem at the top of his lungs. The Henson family gave Libby a Kermit the Frog watch. It is one of those treasures of a lifetime that white suiters cherish.

Roy Adcock in his 1948 Lincoln drives Grand Marshal Kermit the Frog in the 1996 parade

Serving as President of the Tournament of Roses is quite a commitment. Fortunately, most employers in the Pasadena area understand the magnitude of the responsibility and give any employee who rises to that challenge some consideration. Citizens Business Bank was exceptionally supportive: the company gave me a year's leave of absence to complete my assignment. During the year preceding my presidency, Anne and I were gone from home 133 days. I delivered 89 speeches, participated in 112 newspaper interviews, made 25 television appearances, was interviewed on 30 radio talk shows, traveled 77,398 miles, visited 20 states and numerous countries including China and Mexico, took 71 airplane flights, rode in seven parades, and spoke with nine governors.

Our first trip was to Columbus, Indiana, to meet with the Sound of the North Marching Band. Columbus is the headquarters for Cummins International, and one of the highlights of our visit was a tour of the mid-range diesel engine production plant where they supply engines for the nation's Dodge Ram diesel trucks. It was cold in Columbus, and we experienced our first sleet storm. That was the first time I had ever had to scrape ice from our car windows.

Owasso, Oklahoma was next. Their band had been to the Parade three times previously. Anne and I went to the home of Garth Brooks one evening, and had the privilege of meeting his three daughters. What a down-to-earth guy! He was great.

When we visited Carrollton, Georgia, Neil Ruby met us at the Atlanta airport with a limo and three of his students. They presented us with a three-ring binder containing the itinerary for our stay. I think that visit included the most television, radio, and newspaper interviews that I ever had in one place. It was great, and the kids from the band were superb.

My home town is Temple City, and I wanted to make sure that the school my two children had attended would be in the Parade. They never had been, and really were not big enough to qualify at the time. They had 89 players, and would need to grow to the required 150 quickly, still maintaining their quality. The band director, Bert Ferntheil, built his program over a two-year period to meet the Tournament criteria, and they were invited to participate. One day the band was going to play in the local park. They marched down our street and stopped in front of our home to serenade us. Anne had made our yard look just like Parade night, with a fire pit and a sleeping bag

---

This article about the Riffey's visit appeared in a Chinese magazine.

"中国之行令人难忘"

——访美国玫瑰花车协会主席瑞菲先生

□ 本报记者 刘光彩 文/摄

瑞菲(左)与戴维斯在北京合影

春暖花开的日子,美国玫瑰花车协会现任主席瑞菲先生随一50人的大型旅行团访问了中国,同行的还有下届主席戴维斯先生。不少的中国人对每年新年在美国举行的玫瑰花车游行并不陌生,在被世界各地纷纷转播的电视中,我们可以看到,被鲜花装饰的各种各样的大型花车长阵、玫瑰橄榄球队、全美高校乐队依次走过加州绵延十多公里的马路,玫瑰花车公主、演员纷纷在花车上亮相,歌声、笑声、鼓乐声汇成一片,场面十分壮观。

据瑞菲先生介绍,美国一年一度的玫瑰花车游行始于1890年,至今已有一百多年的历史。由最初的2200人参加到现在已经达到上100万人参加的大规模游行,成为美国每年最盛大的新年庆祝活动,也是令世界注目的重大文化活动之一。每年的游行大约有50多个花车,22个乐队,22个骑士。

瑞菲先生说,他和戴维斯先生参加玫瑰花车的游行已有36个年头了,为玫瑰花车协会总部执行委员会的14个成员之一。他们属于自愿者。总部除了22个固定的工作人员外,共有935个志愿者,分属33个委员会,他们每年大约要花8万个小时为这一盛大的节日做准备工作。志愿者最初只是做一些日常的事务工作,逐步升迁

为委员会的负责人。只有在几个委员会做过主席之后,才有可能成为董事会的成员。之后才能进入执行委员会,最终才有资格做一年的主席。整个过程要花费20-30年的时间,并且要牺牲掉无数本该与家人团聚和属于自己的时间。所以能够轮到做主席非常的不容易。按规定,只有主席才有资格穿红色的套服,其他人则穿白色的套服。今年是瑞菲先生做主席,记者采访他时,他特意穿着他的大红套服,显得非常神气。

两位老先生,按中国的习惯,早都过了退休的年纪,可在他们的日程上似乎并没有这项安排,除了作为玫瑰花车执行委员会的成员外,他们一个是银行家,一个是投资顾问,不仅要忙于自己的事务,而且还要负责为玫瑰花车游行筹集资金。他们闲暇时间打高尔夫,钓鱼,整理花园,尽情享受着生活,工作时间则常常工作到很晚,而且经常在空中飞来飞去。

瑞菲先生说:"尽管美伊正发生着战争,许多美国旅游团纷纷取消旅行计划,但我们并没

thrown on the front lawn. The band was great, one of the best on New Year's Day.

Anne and I went to China and Tibet for 19 days with 49 great friends. Dave Davis, who was going to be the President in 2005, and his wife Holly were part of the group. Travelers were worrying about the war in Iraq at the time, as our first day in China was the day the war started. The outbreak of SARS had started, and was spreading throughout China. Reporters consistently asked us why we were there. Our reply was that we had been planning the trip for two and a half years, and we felt very safe in China. We did a lot of flying within the country because it is so large and that is the easiest way to get around. We climbed the Great Wall and saw the Forbidden City, the Temple of Heaven, and the Ming Tomb. We also saw the Terra Cotta Warriors and

spent three days on the Yangtze River. The article about us in the local paper stated, "Mr. Riffey said that he liked China very much. He wishes to introduce the Rose Parade to more Chinese friends and hopes to have more coordination with China in the future." Our party also visited Tibet, where we experienced how very thin the atmosphere is at 11,500 feet elevation.

Our trip to Puebla, Mexico was exciting. We viewed their Cinco de Mayo Parade. They had 37,000 people in their parade! The first 7,000 were military, followed by 26,000 school children, and the rest were rescue units and horse units. We were guests at the Puebla Symphony one evening. They played the *1812 Overture* at the original site of the French war in Mexico. They used probably 250 rifles to simulate the cannon fire. It was quite impressive. We visited churches

and the Piramide de Chulula. At the school over 3,000 students did a beautiful card stunt with fabric on sticks, welcoming us to Mexico. When their band came to Pasadena, they spent two days and nights sleeping on the buses so that they would not have to pay for a hotel. We used Senators and TV stations to get them across the border. The visas were hard to obtain for 280 students.

Another great trip took us to Kahoka, Missouri. Their parade is older than the Rose Parade and they have 2,100 people in the town, which is nicknamed "The Heart of America." The school has 385 students, over half of whom are in the band. What a treat for a small town to come to our Parade!

One final note about the trips takes us to Odessa, Texas. Odessa High School and Permian High School are located in that city. We went to a dinner at

有放弃这次中国之旅,相反,我们认为中国是最安全的地方。"据他介绍,该大型旅游团的52个成员,除了2个因身体的原因取消计划外,其余全部成员按约成行。为了这次旅行,他们在两年半前就开始做准备了。瑞菲先生和戴维斯先生说,对于他们来讲,登中国的长城和去一趟世界屋脊是一生当中最骄傲的事。

他们此次的游程为17天,除了5天在北京外,还将去西安、成都、西藏等地。在北京,他们去了长城、故宫、十三陵、天坛,甚至还看了杂技。令他们感到惊奇的是中国有这么多的人,而且非常友好。过去只是在电视上看到过中国,直到来了之后才知道有多么的不同。他们喜欢北京古老的建筑,在古老的胡同里散步的经历让他们非常难忘。

瑞菲先生说,他很喜欢中国,希望能够将美国的玫瑰花车游行介绍给更多的中国朋友,并希望进一步加强与中国的联系与合作。

 环球访谈

THE RIFFEYS' 2003 TRAVEL LOG

February 13-16 Columbus, Indiana
March 3-6 Owasso, Oklahoma
March 8-10 Santa Clara, California
March 20-April 7 China
April 13-19 Carrollton, Georgia
April 19-27 Charlotte, North Carolina
April 27- May 1 Londonderry,
  New Hampshire
May 4-8 Puebla, Mexico
May 15-20 Ambridge, Pennsylvania
May 22-26 Indianapolis, Indiana
June 5-8 Portland, Alaska

June 11-18 Albuquerque, New Mexico
June 26-30 Boise, Idaho
July 1-8 Cody, Wyoming
July 22-24 Chicago, Illinois
July 24-27 Charlotte, North Carolina
July 27-30 Columbus Ohio
August 5-8 West Des Moines, Indiana
September 17-21 Colorado Springs,
  Colorado
September 25-28 Kahoka, Missouri

the hotel, and during the later part of the evening we were treated to entertainment by the Satin Strings. This is a group of approximately 35 high school students from Permian, playing violins, cellos, harp, and piano. They strolled through the audience and just brought the house down with some great patriotic songs. I turned to Anne and said, "Let's see if we can get them to come to Pasadena and play at the Directors' Dinner!" (That dinner is a black tie event.) They agreed to come, and they took that audience by storm. One of the fellows, strolling among the guests' tables, stopped in front of John Williams, my Grand Marshal, and basically gave a solo performance on one knee. Tears were streaming among the audience members, and the entire group received a standing ovation. The young man who performed for John Williams will never forget the experience. Neither will John. Since the event, the two have communicated with each other. The Satin Strings gave new depth to my "Music, Music, Music" theme. People are still talking about them.

On the morning of "my" Rose Parade, my eyes were open well before the clock radio was supposed to go off. Our normally peaceful house was full to capacity with 14 houseguests. I was prodded by Anne at 3:10 a.m. because ESPN had arrived to do a live interview scheduled for 5 a.m. When asked why they were there so early, they indicated that they had "nothing else to do!" This was a program called *Cold Pizza*, which was to air at 8 a.m. live in New York. By now, the whole house was starting to come alive. Some, including my daughter, were very upset that we had been awakened so early. Everyone started to get ready for the long day ahead. Dave Balfour had arrived at our house at 4:30 a.m. and was to be our official photographer for the balance of the day.

When I walked into our living room, which had been totally dismantled and moved around by the television crew, I was asked to sit down and be wired for the interview. One of the great things that happened was that two of my grandsons got to observe the interview from the satellite truck parked in front of our house. Others watched it live on ESPN in our family room. The interview went well, and by 5:15 a.m. our house had been put back together and the Pasadena Police Department motor officers were standing by to escort us to the Wrigley Mansion.

Upon arrival at the mansion, we were escorted to the dining room for a family breakfast. Special menus had been prepared for the five grandchildren in attendance. Anne's 87 year-old mother was also with us, as she was going to be riding in one of our cars in the parade. It is not a typical practice to have the Tournament President's

On parade morning, Elmo greets one of the Riffey grandchildren.

The beginning of the parade was an emotional moment for Mike and Anne Riffey. At right, Mike Riffey's mother-in-law rides in the parade with the president's family.

PRESIDENT'S FAMILY

PASADENA TOURNAMENT OF ROSES 1987 PRESIDENT SERVES AS GOOD WILL AMBASSADOR IN JORDAN

You're kind of an ambassador when you are representing the United States in another country. Fred W. Soldwedel, President of the 1987 Tournament of Roses, tells a story about his trip. The theme of his parade was "A World of Wonders," and his Grand Marshal was "Pele," the world-renowned soccer player from Brazil. Fred's Music Committee had done a magnificent job of locating bands that had international ties. The Jordanian National Band had applied, and been approved. It is customary for the Tournament President and his wife, if invited, to visit each band before the parade in order to assist with fund-raising, local publicity, parent support, and participant enthusiasm. So, on the invitation of Jordan's band director, Fred and his wife Donna traveled to Jordan for two days in the summer of 1986.

After observing the rehearsals of the band's subdivisions on their first day, they were treated to some sightseeing, complete with driver and interpreter. They visited an ancient Roman ruin and 20th century military sites before lunching on the eastern shore of the Dead Sea. Fred writes,

"In the early afternoon we wound our way through homes tightly clustered up the sides of an impressive mountain to reach the remains of an ancient castle from which the Arabs had watched the approach of the Crusaders centuries before. The view was magnificent. We were the only ones there except for a small group of adults with their children. We crossed the moat, trudged up the surviving castle steps, and climbed over huge toppled stones to arrive at the very uppermost walls. We could see for miles, but only in one direction.

"I noticed that in one outer area you could walk a plank to get a 360° view of the countryside. This I wanted to do. Donna, our driver, and the interpreter remained safely behind. When I returned, I realized I had been watched by all present. A nicely dressed, middle-aged man, one of the other visitors, said something to me in Arabic. I turned to our interpreter and asked

what had been said. Evidently, the man had said that he felt the only reason I was able to make that walk was because I had big feet.

I laughed and raised my foot to show him that I do indeed have big feet. Then, to my horror, I remembered from the few protocol tips a friend had given me that it is very disrespectful in the Arab world to show the sole of one's foot. To make amends, I decided to give all the children a Tournament souvenir. I reached into my pocket and doled out cloissonne rose pins. I noticed that each child would take the pin and show it to his or her father first, even before looking at it. The fathers put the pins in their own pockets, rather than returning them to the children. The man who had commented about my feet was pocketing one pin, and it was my Tournament President's pin!

I had forgotten that earlier in the day I had placed the pin in my pocket for safekeeping. I gestured wildly and took it back. The man had a bewildered look on his face. I thought there might be some kind of confrontation, when out from the crowd stepped a young man who spoke perfect English. He explained to me that he had lived in Glendale, California, sold blue jeans at the Glendale Galleria, and knew about the Parade although he had never seen it. He knew how highly respected the Parade was in the community, and that it would be proper for me to take the pin back. The pin was not mine. It belonged to the Tournament and was mine to wear only so long as I served as President. My new Glendale friend turned around and gave a long, very animated explanation to the father from whom I had taken the pin. When he was through, the Jordanian father said only a few short, rather quiet words, and then there was silence. I broke the silence by asking the interpreter what had been said. Evidently, it had been a simple, somewhat amazed acknowledgement of 'Just think! For a few seconds, I was President of the Tournament of Roses.'

mother-in-law in the parade, but Mom insisted on the privilege and I was glad to comply.

John Pings, who had been assigned to the President's Party from the Television and Radio Committee, had arranged for several television interviews during the morning. When we walked out into the hall after breakfast, we found ourselves face to face with Mickey Mouse. I asked John if he could take Mickey back into the dining room for our grandchildren to enjoy. During one of our trips outside the house, coming back from the KTLA interview, we ran into Elmo. John immediately responded, "I know. You want Elmo in the house, too." The grandkids loved every minute of it.

After breakfast, John Williams and his wife Samantha arrived. Also in attendance were Bill Bogaard, Mayor of Pasadena, Brian Wilson of the Beach Boys, and coming down the staircase was Queen Megan Chinen with her Royal Court. All of a sudden, John Pings announced, "It's time!" and we headed out the front door to our car, a bright yellow 1932 Buick, one of four in the world, worth $1 million. As I put my foot on the running board, 36 years-worth of emotions experienced as a Tournament volunteer flooded over me, and I turned to Anne. Ever my friend and mentor, she instructed, "Don't do that!" I remembered that we had agreed that we would have nothing but fun on this great day, so I smiled and climbed into the car.

It carried us down the Tournament House driveway to our parade route position on Orange Grove Boulevard. As we waited there, I had the opportunity to get out of the car again to visit white suiters, neighbors, and Andy Soucy, music director of the Londonderry High School Band, who had come all the way from New Hampshire to march in the parade.

They finally came to get me as the parade was about to begin. Riding with us for the first time

"One of the more memorable events of my life was attending the Tournament of Roses Parade and the game last year. Uniquely American ... there is nothing like the 'Grandaddy' of them all."
—General Tommy Franks

ever in other cars were my son Todd, his wife April with their children Tyler, Trevor, and Brittany, and my daughter Beth, her husband Todd, and their children Ryan and Smith. Anne's mother Florence was riding with Beth.

The parade was fabulous. The two-hour, ten-minute ride seemed to last about 20 minutes. At the end of the parade, we were met at the Marine Corps Depot by Marine officers and enlisted men in full dress uniform. We had

time to catch our breath until the Queen and her court and Grand Marshal John Williams and his wife Samantha arrived. We had a little refreshment and were then escorted by police convoy to the VIP luncheon next to the Rose Bowl Stadium. There, we were greeted by approximately 2,000 guests of the Tournament who were being entertained by the Ambridge Area High School steel drum band.

The President is given the privilege of inviting 100 personal guests to the parade, luncheon, and game. All of the guests, who included many dignitaries, were awaiting us in the VIP section. Buzz Aldrin, the former astronaut, was there. Air Force General Brian Arnold, Air Force General Hal Hornberg, and our special invited guest Army General Tommy Franks, retired, were all there to greet us.

When lunch was finished, we were taken to the Rose Bowl in golf carts for the pre-game activities. The Rose Bowl was teeming with fans as 93,000 people arrived for the game between USC and Michigan. It was the first time in three years that we had our football partners, the Big Ten and Pac Ten in the Bowl for a traditional match-up. What a thrill it was to walk across the field in this historic stadium with Anne, my son Todd, my daughter Beth, and two great men — John Williams and General Tommy Franks. General Franks would remark later, "One of the more memorable events of my life was attending the Tournament of Ros-

Floats, bands and equestrian units line up in front of the Tournament House and surrounding streets, all ready to begin their entries onto the parade route. Tournament House is at center with green tiled roof.

STEEL DRUMS IN A MARCHING BAND?

We initially thought that the steel drums would ride on a small float, which would be strategically placed in the middle of the band. Bad, bad idea; the Music Committee felt that it would not be safe to put a motorized float anywhere near the band. The drums would have to be pushed or pulled by human power. Back to the drawing board!

My next move was to call Carnegie-Mellon University, which has one of the best engineering schools in the country, to come up with a solution. There was no fooling around, as I went to the best. The head of the engineering department said that there was a senior engineering student who needed a senior project to work on.

After the initial drawings and miniature prototypes, they came up with hand-pushed carts that would hold two people playing single pans, and one-person carts playing multiple pans. After many modifications the carts were completed.

I decided that we needed people with muscle power. Who else would fit the bill, but 14 members of our high school football team? After all the years of playing and cheering in the stands for them, it was payback time.

Our next quest was to find music to play that combines marching band along with steel pans. Since there is no such animal as a marching/steel drum band, there is no music written for marching/steel drum band. I called Dr. Ken Dye, director of the Notre Dame Band and an exceptional composer and arranger. He agreed to arrange the music, and we were well on our way.

After 14 months of fundraising, rehearsals, trials, and tribulations, we were on our way to Pasadena. My assistant and I arrived at the airport early to make sure all the equipment was loaded. We were concerned about the steel drum carts. We had already sent the charter airline a manifest of all our equipment including individual sizes and weights. As they began loading, the gentleman in charge said, "There is no way this is all going to fit!"

I told him, "They have the list, and everything was approved!"

He pulled the list from his notebook and said that the weight was fine, but the dimensions were too big. Mr.

Grueninger, the owner of our tour company, said that he would handle the problem. He then proceeded to call the rental company that had transported the instruments to the airport and told them that we would be needing the rental truck a little longer. He then called his office in Indianapolis and told them to have two drivers ready to drive a truck to California. I was sure that there would be no way that the truck could be there in time for Bandfest, which was in two days.

Sure enough, the equipment made it there in time.

Because we brought our steel drum band with us, the band staff was kept very busy with three steel drum performances and two marching band performances. The marching band had Bandfest and the Parade, while the steel drums entertained all the sponsors of the Tournament of Roses at a cocktail party, the band directors, dignitaries, and Mr. John Williams at the band directors' brunch, and finally all of the VIPs before game time.

On the day of the parade, our schedule was very different from most bands' because of the steel drum involvement. We had the equipment truck that carried the steel drums and carts leave first at 4:00 a.m., then the steel drum players at 4:30 a.m., and finally the rest of the band at 5:00 a.m. As the band boarded the bus, I received a call from my assistant, who was with the steel drum players. He thought he had seen our equipment truck stopped in the middle of the freeway.

Sure enough, the truck had broken down. We pulled all of our buses to the side of the freeway to investigate.

When we arrived at the line-up site, the Tournament officials already knew of our predicament and assured me that all would be well. There was no time to get another truck and reload the equipment, so they had ordered a tow truck to tow the equipment, truck and all, to the lineup area, escorted by the California Highway Patrol.

Another obstacle had been overcome and although my heart had become a little weaker, our performance was a smashing success and an experience of a lifetime.

—Sal Aloe
Ambridge Area High School Band Director

es Parade and the game last year. Uniquely American . . . there is nothing like the 'Grandaddy of them all.'"

Arriving from 3,500 feet were the "Wings of Blue," the US Air Force Academy's jump team. They flew in the game ball, the coin to be tossed by John Williams, and the American flag. All of the jumpers landed perfectly in the center of the field, and then presented the above-mentioned items to John and me.

I had asked John when he was selected as Grand Marshal if he would conduct both of the university bands playing the National Anthem before the game. Without anybody's knowledge, John created his own arrangement of the piece, and it was played that day. At specific times all 93,000 attendees participated in a card stunt that showed two American flags running end to end throughout the whole stadium. The stealth bombers flew over at the prescribed time, hailed with a fanfare of fireworks. And then the game began.

After a thrilling game, I presented to Pete Carroll, coach of the USC Trojans, the Rose Bowl Trophy. USC had defeated Michigan 28 – 14. Anne and I were then escorted by the police to an After Game Supper at the Tournament House, held to thank the committee chairs and the three float judges for a job magnificently done.

Aguiluchos marching band drill team members march proudly in costumes inspired by their homeland. The band is from the Centro Escolar Niños Chapultepec, Puebla, Mexico.

At about 7:30 p.m. it was time to leave and go home to our houseguests. As soon as I greeted them, I excused myself and retired from a very long day. As far as I was concerned, January 1, 2004 had been the most perfect day in the world.

I wanted my tenure as 2004 President and Chairman of the Board of the Tournament of Roses (my heart still thrills when I see that title on my business cards!) to bring fresh ideas and new traditions to the Tournament. New Year's Day 2004 brought the largest band in the parade's history, 530-strong, a combined band of

Odessa High School and Permian High School from Odessa, Texas. They reserved the entire Marriott Hotel in Orange County for their stay.

Steel drums, pushed by a contingent of football players plus the balance of the band from Ambridge Area High School, Ambridge, Pennsylvania, joined the parade for the first time.

For the first time ever, a band from our neighbor to the south, Aguiluchos marching band, Centro Escolar Ninos Heros Chapultepec, from Puebla, Mexico, joined us. They wore brand new uniforms that were unique and very

CLASSIC AUTOMOBILES CARRY PARADE DIGNITARIES

During the initial·trials in December, "Our big '27 Touring Eight never got above 165 degrees," he crows. I met Dan in 2001 at the CCCA Grand Classic show in Pasadena, where I approached him about driving the car in the 2004 parade and assured him that Els Hazenberg would be extremely careful of its finish when she decorated it. "There's more paint were that came from," Dan grinned. In his article, he shares a few moments of terror at the start of the parade, when someone noticed that coolant was leaking from under the car. Dan grabbed his cell phone and called an expert, who calmly attributed the leakage to overflow, and the rising temperature gauge to a "true temperature" reading as opposed to the usual reading from vapors. Sure enough, once the overflow was gone, the car settled in and performed beautifully. Dan says that the brass 2004 Tournament of Roses bumper badge given to him for the parade is still proudly mounted on the car.

striking, all because Anne had encouraged them to choose uniforms that reflected their national personality.

Other "firsts" that day included: The program covers and the Tournament poster bore different designs.

For the first time in the Parade's history, the President's family rode in three separate cars: a 1931 Buick (one of four remaining in the entire world!), a 1936 Packard Phaeton, and a 1927 Packard 343 Seven Passenger Touring Sedan. The latter car was written up in the spring 2004 edition of *Packards International Magazine* by Keith Alber, who interviewed Dan Murphy, the owner and driver of the car. Alber's article conveys Dan's enthusiasm for the Rose Parade adventure.

For the first time in history, the Grand Marshal conducted the bands from the opposing universities' teams as they played the Star Spangled Banner together.

For the first time in history, the parade's Grand Marshal arranged the National Anthem for the Rose Bowl Game.

Rose Parade flyovers began in 1912, when C. P. Rogers, who had made the first transcontinental airplane flight, flew over the parade route sprinkling rose petals from the sky. No rose petals rained on the 2004 parade, but the flyover was unique — three stealth planes were allowed by a one-day special order to fly in formation: an F-117A Nighthawk, an F/A-22 Raptor, and a B-2 Stealth Bomber. The B-2 leaves very early New Year's morning from Whiteman Air Force Base in Missouri, flies over the parade, and then goes out for a training mission and comes back to fly over the game. They then head home, never setting down.

At the end of the parade, there was a second flyover, which is another "first." The helicopters from the firefighters' association flew over at the end of the parade.

And finally, for the first time ever, the official parade souvenir pin was three-dimensional: a tiny tambourine with moving jingles.

"WE'LL BE THERE."

The 1997 parade was the first time parade audiences saw the "bat-winged" B-2 Stealth Bomber. Paul Holman was the chair of the Public Relations Committee that year and was responsible for the Press Stand at the corner of Orange Grove and Colorado Boulevard. About three days before the parade, Paul received a late-evening call from an Air Force major, who said that a Tournament staff member had referred him to Paul. He asked Paul to help him find a camera location so they could film the flyover. He explained that, for promotional purposes, they wanted to film the B-2 flying over the Air Force Band as it turned the corner.

Paul and his committee found some suitable camera locations and showed them to the major. "Now, all I need to know is when the Air Force Band will be halfway around the corner," he stated. Paul thought for a moment, retrieved his parade timing sheet from his briefcase, and did a few calculations. He responded, "The band will be halfway around the corner at about 8:06."

Paul describes the next interaction thus: "The major stared at me for a moment. Then, with a look on his face somewhere between patience and pity, he simply said, 'I didn't say about.' I looked at him for a long moment, my mind slowly 'getting it.' I went back to the timing sheet, got out my calculator, and did the math. At the same time, I was mentally listing all the things that could go wrong to make my calculations useless. I finally said, 'The Air Force Band will be halfway around the corner at 8:06 and 37 seconds, IF …' and then proceeded to list all the things that could go wrong: a late start, slow units in front, band spacing, etc. etc. The major quietly responded, 'We'll be there.'"

On parade day Paul waited on top of the press stand at the corner with a digital watch, set precisely to parade time. He had shared the above story with some committee members who stood with him. They faced west, spotting the slim profile of the B-2 as it approached. "He's going to be too far north!," one exclaimed. The B-2 banked sharply to the right, lining up exactly with Colorado Boulevard. Another said, "He's going too fast!" Paul could see the ailerons on the B-2's wings opening and closing, slowing the plane down. The band approached the corner as the B-2 came closer. As the band reached halfway around the corner, the B-2 reached the spot for the photograph. Paul's watch read 8:06:37. Paul called out the time, and the man next to him muttered, "Man, am I glad they're on our side!"

That morning my alarm did not go off, and I woke up seven minutes after we were supposed to have left. I remember thinking to myself, "The one day I get to be on world-wide television, I wake up late and don't have time to do my hair!"

I was the drum major for a band in the biggest parade in the world, the Rose Parade, every drum major's dream.

At a breakfast at Pasadena College, I learned all about the way the Parade works. After the meal and the meeting were over, they gave everyone a drum. Then one person led us through an event called a drum circle. I can still remember the sounds of all the drums, people making up rhythms and playing them at the same time, yet its sounding as if we were following a written piece of music. It gave me the chills.

Another wonderful event was the luncheon at the Ritz Carlton. At this meal, I got to meet several other drum majors, the Rose Queen and Princesses, and even the Grand Marshal, John Williams.

I left the luncheon to head for the NBC press box to record a circle-wide to be shown as my band marched through the television zone on New Year's Day. I did

three takes with the beautiful California mountains in the background. This was a very memorable moment for me, because I realize that not everyone can say they have talked on world-wide television before.

My band did so many fun things while we were in California. We went to Universal Studios, Disneyland, a dinner cruise, a show at the Crystal Cathedral, the Santa Monica Pier, and the Farmer's Market. We shared so much fun together. It was a great way to strengthen relationships among our band members.

The day of the Parade, we had to get up at 3:30 a.m. to get in line for the Parade. We sat on the bus for almost two and a half hours. The bus was completely silent because everyone was asleep. I woke up once for a little while and just sat there thinking about what a great memory I was about to experience. I reflected on all the hard work and dedication it had taken to get to the spot we were in. I knew that I didn't want to forget anything about that day.

When everyone started waking up, you could feel the excitement growing and growing. As soon as I stepped off the bus, I whispered softly to myself, "This is it!" It was what I had been waiting for for so long.

As we rushed to get everything off the bus and run up the hill and line up in three minutes, the anticipation of what lay ahead kept getting stronger. We lined up the band in our parade formation after many people made pit-stops at the Porta-Potties. We warmed up, and then the Parade began.

I was amazed at all the people lined up along the road and sitting in the stands! Millions of spectators watched as we marched and played *Georgia on My Mind.* I remember certain spectators who touched my heart. Right before I turned the corner onto Colorado Boulevard, there was a row of military men sitting together. As drum major, I was saluting the cameras and viewers. As I was saluting, I saw the row of men and made eye contact with them. At that moment, all of them saluted me back and gave me huge smiles.

It seemed as if we were never going to be done with the parade. It just kept going and going. About halfway through the five and a half miles, we were surprised by many of our supporters, chaperones, and family members cheering us on. When there was only one mile left, a crowd member held up a sign that read, "One mile left!" Oh, the happiness that I felt when I read that! Every quarter mile from there to the end, someone held up a sign telling us how much farther we had until the end.

When we finally reached the end, I was so happy, but then again I was sad, too. It was over. All that training and getting ready for that day, that Parade, didn't matter any more because it was all over.

Mr. and Mrs. Riffey are the absolute best. They took time to come and visit the bands' hometowns. I consider their visit to Carrollton, Georgia, a great honor. They came to several of our performances and practices and even went with me and a few others to talk about the Parade on the best radio station in Atlanta. They made me feel like a very important part of the Parade.

The 2004 Rose Parade was one of the best trips of my life. I know that I will never have a more memorable experience.

—Kris Powers, Age 17
Drum Major
Central Carroll High School

The Goodyear blimp, long a fixture in Tournament of Roses history, floats high above Tournament House on parade morning.

Mike and Anne Riffey visit the float barn where volunteers are busy decorating the entries for the parade.

The crowds file past the queue of floats to find curb-side places along the route. The best seats go early!

Boy and Girl Scouts are in charge of the prize winning float banners. The banners are hung in order of the parade and pairs of scouts proceed them with the appropriate banner.

Scouts carry the President's Trophy banner awarded for best floral presentation, in 2005.

CHAPTER 3

Settings

Pre-parade festivities at the Tournament House are reflected in this tuba.

Settings

Even if you can't be with us physically for the Tournament, it might help you to picture the whole operation better if you knew a bit of our architectural and historical geography.

The center of operations for the Pasadena Tournament of Roses is the Tournament House, also known as the Wrigley mansion. The official brochure put out by the association describes it as "a stately three-story, 22-room, 18,500 square-foot Italian Renaissance-style mansion." It is situated about two city blocks south of the western end of Colorado Boulevard. Except for New Year's Eve and the day of the parade, its grounds are open to the public year-round.

I have heard that, in its day, the mansion was considered "modest" in size and design. That adjective makes me smile. If this mansion is modest, smite me with a modest home! Laura, my faithful writer, told me when she first saw it that it reminded her of the George Eastman House in Rochester, New York, which she visited often as a child. Such houses are part of our national heritage, born in an era when it wasn't unusual to find a back staircase in a home for use by the live-in servants.

The mansion was built on South Orange Grove Boulevard (nicknamed "Millionaire's Row") starting in 1906. In those days, the magnificent homes on the boulevard were used as winter retreats by Midwestern and Eastern industrialists. G. Lawrence Stimson was the mansion's architect, and his father, George W. Stimson, was its builder. The elder Stimson was a real estate and dry goods tycoon. They constructed the building to last, using poured concrete and steel; the process took eight years!

The front door of the mansion is ornately carved from four-inch-thick Honduras mahogany, just one example of the elegant details that make the mansion so solidly beautiful. While the door is extremely heavy, it was installed to be perfectly balanced and can be moved with just the slightest touch.

Mr. Stimson believed firmly that landscaping, particularly trees, would help increase a property's value, and he hired an English gardener to collect and plant specimen trees from around the world to enhance his estate. The region was naturally barren at the time; the Pasadena climate is, after all, arid. The front lawn was originally planted with so

many palms that the subsequent owner, Mrs. Wrigley, nicknamed her home "The Shadows," but a wind storm in the 1930s destroyed most of the trees that had hidden the home from the street for more than a decade. South of the porch in the front garden is the showpiece of Stimson's collection of trees, a Moreton Bay Fig. This type of tree, given the right climate and conditions, will grow to become one of the largest trees in the world. (The largest of these trees in the United States is in Lahaina on the island of Maui, Hawaii.)

By the time the home was finished, most of the Stimson children had grown and moved away. Mr. and Mrs. Stimson found the house much too large for their needs, and in 1914 sold the house to William Wrigley, Jr., for $170,000. A year later, Wrig-

ley purchased adjoining property on the north side for $25,000. He razed the house on that property and brought in an arbor and colorful roses to create a formal garden which remains today as the most extensive rose garden on the grounds.

The Wrigley family watched the Pasadena Rose Parade every New Year's from the front of their beautiful home. I like to imagine their walking out of that massive front door and down the two-inch-thick Italian marble steps of the entrance. I fancy their sitting in padded wicker chairs and drinking hot chocolate or steaming coffee, waited upon by servants who lived on the third floor of the mansion. The parade originally began two blocks north (toward the mountains) in front of the house at the corner of Ellis and Orange Grove. Nowa-

days, on the night before the parade, floats fill the boulevard for 13 blocks. The bands and equestrian units enter from side streets across from the house.

Much of the beautiful woodwork in the interior of the Tournament House is irreplaceable, as it is crafted of woods that are now extinct. The living room features matched doors of Circassian Walnut from Romania. The Florentine Italian marble fireplace at the south end of the living room was ordered from a catalog and shipped through the E. V. Collins Marble Company of Los Angeles and assembled on site. Just as assembly was about to begin, however, the builder discovered that the marble company forgot to enclose assembly instructions. Sending to Italy for the plans delayed installation. When the mansion was renovated, the cherry wood fireplace mantel in the library was recreated using 25 different pieces of molding to replicate the original mantel that the Wrigleys enjoyed on cold winter nights. The library also showcases one of the design elements that made Stimson famous as an architect — the ornate molded plaster ceiling now known as a "Stimson" ceiling.

The Pasadena home was one of six the Wrigleys owned; the others were in Philadelphia, Chicago, Phoenix, Lake Geneva (Wisconsin), and at Avalon on Catalina Island, 20 miles off the coast of Los Angeles. After William Wrigley Jr.'s death in 1932, Pasadena became his widow's favorite residence. After her death in 1958, the family presented the property and the furniture it contained to the City of Pasadena, requesting that it become the permanent base of operations

Clockwise from left: This portrait of the 1907 Rose Queen, Joan Hadenfeldt Woodbury hangs in the dining room. The dining room decorated for New Year's morning breakfast. The dining room is furnished with pieces from the era of the Wrigley's residence at Tournament House.

for the Tournament of Roses Association. The city leased it to the Tournament for 50 years, starting in 1959, for a fee of $50. Offices and a large downstairs room were added on to the structure in 1960 for use by year-round staff.

I enjoy showing visitors what has been affectionately dubbed the "Eisenhower bathroom." It seems that, in 1963, while serving as Rose Parade Grand Marshal, the former President of the United States became trapped by the bathroom's recessed sliding door just before the parade was to begin. The sounds of the morning parade drowned out poor Ike's pounding for several minutes, until he was finally rescued.

The room south of the library, often referred to as the solarium or sun porch, was originally built as an open garden balcony. It featured a concrete bow-front balustrade and steps leading down to a reflecting pool and garden. The garden was replaced with a terrace to better accommodate the current use of the house.

The Tournament House's formal dining room is the only room in the house that is furnished with pieces from the Wrigley era. The hand-carved Italian dining room table, 12 chairs, and two sideboards were originally purchased for this house, shipped to the Wrigley house on Catalina Island, and then returned to Pasadena to prevent damage from Catalina's moist island air. Figured Crotch Mahogany from the Philippines lines the dining room walls. The panels' color has

darkened with age, providing a rich background for the alabaster chandelier and matching wall sconces. Every visitor comments about the striking oil painting of Joan Hadenfeldt Woodbury, 1907's Rose Queen.

Many interesting items are displayed throughout the first and second floors of the mansion.

The "Eisenhower bathroom" where, in 1963, the former President became trapped before the parade.

These include a one-of-a-kind Waterford crystal bowl commissioned for the 100th Celebration, a portrait of the current Rose Queen by the Charis Studio in Pasadena, and a variety of historical sterling silver trophies, as well as vintage accoutrements, souvenirs, and photographs. When the Wrigleys were in residence, the second floor consisted of a spa-

cious book-lined central hall surrounded by five bedrooms and four baths, plus a sleeping porch. Today, the hallway is lined with beautiful glass-paneled wood trophy displays. Visitors are delighted by memorabilia from past Rose Bowl games, the Queens and their Courts, Grand Marshals, and Tournament Presidents.

The Queen and Court's Room, which is located on the second floor facing Orange Grove Boulevard, seems a serene oasis of striped mint green walls, rose-accented upholstery and chintz suitable for a Queen and her Royal Court. Outside the room is a lighted, velvet-lined display of historical crowns and tiaras. What a hive of activity this room becomes at three o'clock in the morning on Parade day! The girls come freshly showered, with wet hair, in their pajamas. They are then coiffed, made up, given breakfast, and helped with their gowns by a staff of skilled volunteers.

The structure opposite the driveway on the north side of the house is the garage that housed the Wrigleys' cars. It boasted its own hydraulic hoist for lifting the cars for repairs. At its northwest corner is a tree known as "The Freedom Tree." It is a *Mela Leuca Linariifolia*, commonly known as "Snow In Summer," and was planted on May 19, 1973 to honor Pasadena resident Warrant Officer James A. Johansen and all others killed in the Vietnam War. The building to the west of the garage is the Tournament Annex, which houses restrooms, show-

THE ROYALS FLUSH?

After the Queen and Court's Room was redecorated, a committeeman with a well-known paper company presented us with 100 rolls of toilet tissue, with a large red rose imprinted on each sheet. The pretty tissue made the four stalls in the restroom very colorful. The rolls of tissue started to disappear very quickly, and shortly all 100 rolls were gone! A committee man observed that the seven girls must use the restroom a lot, and wondered how they would manage the five-and-a-half mile Parade on January first. Did they have a personal problem?

After questioning the girls we discovered that they had been quietly taking the rolls of tissue home as souvenirs.

— Alexander H. Gaal
San Marino, CA

ers, and staff quarters; it is used by Tournament volunteers who work through the night on New Year's Eve.

The grounds of the mansion are now maintained by the Tournament of Roses Association. Volunteers from the Pacific Rose Society care for the rose gardens. The walkway to the south garden passes a bench commemorating the 75th Rose Parade. On January 2, 1989, the Association celebrated its 100th Rose Parade and 75th Rose Bowl Game. The parking lot to the west was once the site of the Wrigleys' tennis court. The executive offices that can be viewed from the south garden were added by the Tournament of Roses Association in 1960 and remodeled in 1987. At the center of the south rose garden is a fountain, which was created in honor of the Centennial. A time capsule, which contains memorabilia from 1989 rests beneath the plaque at the fountain's center and will be opened in 2089 when the Tournament of Roses celebrates its Bicentennial. The roses planted around the fountain were developed by the Jackson & Perkins Company, the world's largest producer of roses, and are named "Tournament of Roses" as the official rose of the Centennial. This coral-pink variety was one of only four roses to win the prestigious All-America Rose Selections award in 1989. The All-America Rose Selections' test gardens contain hundreds of varieties of roses, camellias, and annuals. The gardens are open to the public throughout the year except for December 31 through January 2. They are the backdrop for many special events each year, from the selection and announcement of the Rose Queen and Royal Court, to the announcement of each year's Grand Marshal.

Renovated over a period of three years from 2000 to 2002 with the help of the Pasadena Chapter of the American Society of Interior Designers (ASID) and a local contractor, The Tournament House is now staffed by 21 full-time employees; it is the base of operations for the Tournament's 935 dedicated volunteers. The employees share the volunteers' passion for the Tournament, and one senses an almost protective tone in their voices when they talk about it. We have all become great friends over the years, and many of them have contributed important information for this book. Some of the stories on earlier days, for example, came from Jack French. Jack was the Tournament CEO for approximately 16 years, from June of 1984 to February of 2000. He served as Executive Director from May of 1981 to June of 1996. He is still involved with the Tournament and runs some of our major grandstands. He is under contract and sells those seats every year to the public. Jack was also a Tournament member for some 10 years preceding his tenure as CEO. His name is really John H. B. French, but we have called him Jack forever.

One office in the new section of the Tournament House is reserved for the use of the President of the Tournament. Two large glass cases in the Rose Room hold the wonderful gifts that the President and his or her spouse receive during the year in office. Anne and I have, of course, become very familiar with both the mansion and the staff, and each of us feels a touch of humility and pride each time we walk along the pathways to the building's entrance. What energy, dedication, creativity, and sheer hard work are brought to focus within those walls!

About two blocks toward the San Gabriel Mountains and the 210 freeway from the Tournament House, Orange Grove Boulevard intersects with Colorado Boulevard. Orange Grove Boulevard is a city street, and Colorado Boulevard is a state highway, which means that different types of permits must be obtained to use the intersecting thoroughfares. The right turn from Orange Grove onto Colorado is a 109° turn; in other words, it's an unusually tight right turn and drivers have to cramp the steering wheel hard to the right in order to steer around it. Most floats are now 55 feet in length, so the drivers really have to know what they're doing. The Tournament assists them with a Turning Crew. Each member of the crew has a visual of what the float looks like, and a diagram of the locations of its wheels, its tow bars and its fire extinguishers. They know exactly what its turning radius is, and help to guide the observer and the driver at the turn. One year I was on the Turning Crew and turned the St. Louis float, which is pulled by eight Clydesdale horses. It was a 55-foot float. I asked the driver if he would have trouble making the left hand turn. He said to point him in the direction we wanted him to go, and he would make the corner. He did, with ease.

A number of years ago the Casablanca Fan Company float, which had a live circus act on it, also had a live Bengal tiger chained to the front of the float with a very short chain. When the 55-foot float tried to turn the corner at Orange Grove and Colorado, it turned so tight that the top part of the float got hung up on the traffic signal. It was stalled from some ten minutes with the tiger virtually in the laps of many parade viewers. That signal is removed now, each year, and must be replaced within four hours of the completion of the parade.

Immediately on the left (north) side of Colorado after the turn, right across the street from Stephanie Edwards' and Bob Eubank's lofty perch above the grandstands, lies the Norton Simon Museum. The museum wall is graced each year by a huge copy of the Tournament's logo rose. The logo was designed in 1983 by Susan Karasic, a student at the Art Center College of Design in Pasadena. Larry Crain's crew at Charisma Floats decorates the 15-foot diameter piece each year with carnations and lemon leaf petals and hangs it in place to greet the nation and the world.

Further on down Colorado the Parade turns onto Sierra Madre Boulevard, which is a divided street with an

This large, petal bedecked rose logo is hung each year on the wall of the Norton Simon Museum.

A beautiful sunrise greets people finding their seats in the stands, as thousands of others stream toward vantage points along Orange Grove and Colorado Boulevards.

island. On one occasion, a float driver told Tournament officials emphatically that he did not need help turning the corner, even though he did not have vision to the front of the float. He ultimately ran into the crowd as he turned left onto Sierra Madre. When we opened the hatch to talk with him, we found that he had his girlfriend in that tiny compartment with him. Enough said.

At the Paseo Colorado Shopping Center, special services are available for handicapped members of the parade audience. The Tournament provides Braille Institute prints and programs written in Braille. Volunteers are available to sign for deaf observers. Another of these centers is available at the end of the parade route.

On Colorado Boulevard there is a bridge between St. John and Pasadena Avenues. The Tournament asks marching bands to refrain from high stepping as they cross the bridge, as 300 marchers' high stepping causes the bridge to vibrate. The grandstands are portable, and they line the entire bridge on both sides of the street. Once, a long time ago, a stand collapsed from the vibration. Once is more than enough to have that happen!

This young man emerges from the cramped driver's compartment of a float after the 1990 Parade.

THE LONDONDERRY MARCHING LANCERS

I witnessed the elegance and grandeur of the Rose Parade in 1997, when my daughter Jennifer, a freshman piccolo player with the Londonderry Marching Lancers, was marching, and then again in 2004 with two new friends, Mike and Anne Riffey, the Tournament of Roses President and his wife.

During the 1997 visit, I climbed onto the press photographers' scaffolding on the corner of Orange Grove Boulevard and Colorado Boulevard to cover the event for our town's local newspapers. Growing up, I had always been amazed at how the enormous floats and bands made their way around the 109° turn with ease while I watched the Parade on television. It was surreal to be at "the turn" and be able to witness it in person.

Rain is a rarity in the history of the Parade, which has seen rain only nine times in its history. Throughout the night before the Parade, there were light rain showers. And then the sun rose, almost on cue, and began to break through the clouds. The skies turned a magical purple and blue color, with highlights of golden yellow and orange. These were the same colors that I would see in a few hours on each of the flower-decorated floats. As the crowd observed the sunrise, a cheer began through the stadium seats lined up along Colorado Boulevard. Once again, the Tournament of Roses Executive Vice President had fulfilled his job. He had brought good weather for the Parade.

Since this was my first visit, I was excited and a bit overwhelmed. I had my press credentials around my neck and was greeted at the towering scaffolding by the Tournament White Suiter officials, who escorted me to where I would take my pictures. I climbed three levels of scaffolding and was treated as if I were a regular fixture among some of the country's biggest newspapers, magazines, and news crews.

The air was full of electricity as thousands of people passed below me on the way to their assigned seats. I had no idea what to expect, but was given some advice from fellow photographers who had been to the Parade before. Since the scaffolding would be crowded, the other photographers would step aside and allow me the necessary space to cover the event when the Lancers marched through the turn. I had a job to do, but also wanted to focus on my daughter as she marched by. I could only imagine the 5.5 mile journey that was ahead of her and the other band members.

At approximately 8:00 a.m., the streets were cleared of people and the Pasadena motorcycle entourage began to lead the Parade participants down Orange Grove Boulevard. The United States Marine Band began the Parade, and, without warning, a stealth bomber flew overhead. The Parade was officially underway.

Within the hour, the Lancers appeared and my camera never stopped clicking. The moment I saw my daughter, holding her head high and piccolo straight as she had been instructed to do, time stood still and a wave of pride and emotion stole the moment. When the Lancers turned the corner and were marching out of sight, I made my way down the scaffolding and just stared down Colorado Boulevard at the backs of their uniforms as they made their way onward.

During my second visit to the Rose Parade, I received another special memory from "the turn." Mike Riffey yelled up to me as he rode with Anne in a 1932 yellow Buick Victoria convertible and pointed behind him toward the Lancers with his thumb up.

Since this was my second visit I was able to take a deeper look behind the scenes that had been a blur during my first visit. From the hustle and bustle of the pre-Parade activities to the immense amount of security, there were so many details! The equestrian street sweepers decorated their shovels and brooms with roses and adorned their white overalls with corsages and boutonnieres, and the White Suiters paid special attention to make sure that all of the spectators got to their assigned seats in time for the step-off. It was truly a masterful symphony of hard work and joy, blended in harmony to help everyone enjoy the year's theme: Music, Music, Music.

— Bob Ross
Londonderry Marching Band and Colorguard
Friends of Music

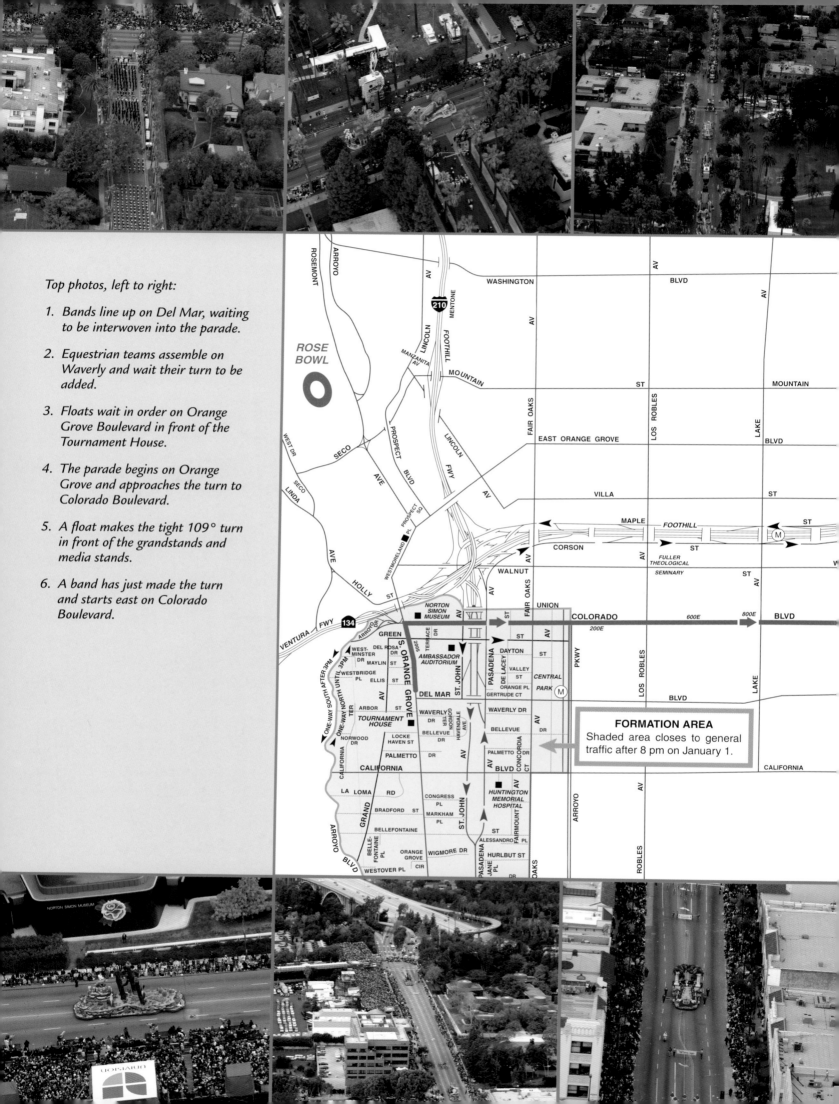

Top photos, left to right:

1. *Bands line up on Del Mar, waiting to be interwoven into the parade.*

2. *Equestrian teams assemble on Waverly and wait their turn to be added.*

3. *Floats wait in order on Orange Grove Boulevard in front of the Tournament House.*

4. *The parade begins on Orange Grove and approaches the turn to Colorado Boulevard.*

5. *A float makes the tight 109° turn in front of the grandstands and media stands.*

6. *A band has just made the turn and starts east on Colorado Boulevard.*

FORMATION AREA
Shaded area closes to general traffic after 8 pm on January 1.

POST - PARADE AREA

Floats will be displayed along Sierra Madre Blvd between Paloma St and Sierra Madre Villa Av and along Washington Blvd between Sierra Madre Blvd and Woodlyn Rd.

Tournament of Roses Parade Route

Bottom photos, left to right:

7. A float rolls past the media and is seen in front of the Norton Simon Museum. This is view that most TV broadcasts show to the world.

8. There's a long way to go from here. Beyond the corner, the Colorado Boulevard Bridge spans Arroyo Seco where, to the north, the Rose Bowl Stadium sits.

9. Midway through downtown Pasadena are the Queen's float and hearlds.

10. The Pasadena Motorcycle Police perform a precision routine on the route.

11. On the route looking east.

12. Parade's over! Spectators begin walking down Colorado Boulevard after the last of the entries.

CHAPTER 4

Move Over, Pasadena!

Move Over, Pasadena!

Any enterprise that brings hundreds of thousands of people to a single location and thrives on the efforts of thousands of volunteers has to be organized around rules and regulations that protect the well-being of all concerned.

Let me give you an example of what I'm talking about. In 1981, a float was being pulled by a team of mules owed by a fellow by the name of Smizer. Now Mr. Smizer was an experienced mule team driver, but he had had back surgery six months prior to the parade. The braking system on the float required that a foot brake be applied by pressing down. Mr. Smizer felt that he would be able to use the brake, but he had a fellow riding "shotgun" with him, just in case. Unfortunately, as it turned out, his shotgun rider only weighed about 100 pounds soaking wet. Tournament rules, however, require that any horse- or mule-drawn vehicle have a backup battery-powered braking system, in case anything goes wrong. So the float proceeded down Colorado Boulevard on schedule. When it hit the downhill stretch the mules began pulling too fast and the drivers tried to apply the brakes, but they were unable to counter the float's momentum. The float swerved to the left, passing a band and another float as it gained speed. Eventually Mr. Smizer was able to get his team stopped, then went on down the Parade route as if nothing had happened. That night, float officials examined the float and found that the back-up battery had not been re-charged per Tournament rules.

TOURNAMENT COMMITTEES

Communications and Credentials: Manages telephone and radio communications prior to and during the Rose Parade. Secures and distributes Rose Parade credentials. Works with the Tournament of Roses Radio Amateurs.

Community Relations: Serves as a speaker's bureau of behalf of the Associatio in representation to community organizations, schools, churches, and clubs.

Coronation/VIP Tailgate: Handles all arrangements for the Coronation Ceremony of the Rose Queen and Royal Court, and for the Royal Ball held in honor of all Queen and Court tryout participants., Plans and hosts the Tournament's guests at a tailgate party immediately following the Rose Parade.

Decorating Places: Manages the public viewing for the various float building locations., Handles all arrangements for planning the viewing sites. Acts as hosts to the public and maintains the safety and security at these locations.

Equestrian: Invites and coordinates the participation of the Rose Parade's equestrian entries. Plans and hosts the Equestrian Reception. Organizes the annual Equestfest.

Fanfest: Responsible for planning Fanfest, the activity-filled event that takes place outside the Rose Bowl stadium during the days leading up to the New Year.

Float Construction: Supervises construction of all floats and verifies compliance with all.

Float Entries: Invites and coordinates participation of the Rose Parade's float entries. Maintains year-round contact with float participants.

Food Services: Hosts the annual Tournament of Roses membership kickoff event. Provides food to Tournament workers and Parade participants on New Year's Eve and New Year's Day.

Football: Maintains year-round contact with NCAA officials and the participating colleges and universities.

Formation Area: Secures the Rose Parade Formation Area and works with law enforcement to maintain crowd control in that area from New Year's Eve through the duration of the Rose Parade.

Heritage: Provides coordination to preserve Tournament of Roses heritage and historical artifacts. Duties include managing and conducting house tours and managing the Tournament of Roses museum.

Host: Provides and coordinates hosting activites for Executive Committee invited participants, sponsors, and special guests. Manages the Grand Marshal party and the official President's party.

Judging: Selects, invites, and escorts Rose Parade float judges to judging sites. Announces the float award winners on New Year's morning.

Kickoff Events/Hall of Fame: Oversees the staging of the Rose Bowl Game Kickoff Luncheon, the event honoring the teams playing in the Game and attended by the Grand Marshal, Rose Queen, Tournament and university officials, players, and coaches. Plans and coordinates all Hall of Fame activities.

Liaison and Planning: Serves as liaison between the city of Pasadena, other agencies, and Tournament committees for compliance with all rules, regulations, and ordinances.

Membership Development: Develops membership recruitment programs. Helps to establish objectives and actions to enhance communication with members to ensure their continued interest in the Tournament.

Music: Invites and serves as liaison to each of the Rose Parade's marching bands. Stages the Tournament's annual Bandfest.

Parade Operations: Oversees operations from the beginning of the Rose Parade, including timing and uninterrupted flow over the 5 _ mile route.

Post Parade: Receives floats at the Post Parade display area. Coordinates public viewing of the floats after the Rose Parade at the Post Parade Showcase of Floats.

Press Photo/Trophy: Greets and assists media at the Rose Parade. Organizes and hosts two official press stands during the Parade. Hosts VIP grandstands and portable stands. Provides participation trophies to each Rose Parade float and band.

Queen and Court: Conducts the interview leading to the selection of the Rose Queen and Royal Court. Escorts court members to all appearances after their selection.

Services and Properties: Contracts all security personnel and portable facilities for Tournament of Roses events. Maintains an accurate inventory of all equipment used for each Rose Parade.

Special Events: Organizes and implements Tournament of Roses special events as assigned.

Sports Media: Hosts and operates central press headquarters for members of the media covering the Rose Bowl Game.

Student Ambassadors: Oversees the Student Ambassador program for high school volunteers, identifies and recommends activities, chaperones the students at each event and acts as day-to-day liaison with the students, school officials, and Tournament officials.

Television and Radio: Acts as liaison with all radio and television outlets providing live coverage of the Rose Parade. Coordinates Parade route positions for each outlet.

Tournament Auxiliary: A ready reserve of retired Tournament members providing assistance to committees in the months leading up to the New Year's Day festivities.

Tournament Entries: Selects and coordinates Rose Parade vehicles used by the Grand Marshal, Tournament President, Rose Queen and Royal Court, and Mayor of Pasadena. Responsible for placement of float award banners. Provides security on Tournament House grounds between December 26 and January 1.

Tournament Grandstands: Hosts the Tournament's distinguished Rose Parade guests on New Year's Day. Hosts grandstands for mobility impaired viewers.

Transportation: Provides transportation for Tournament of Roses officials, distinguished guests , and game participants. Issues official vehicles.

University Entertainment: Hosts the visiting football teams and other representatives of the participating colleges and universities in the Rose Bowl Game.

As various problems and crises have presented themselves over the years, those who oversee the Tournament have written handbooks and regulations aimed at preventing such difficulties from recurring in the future. The body that manages the entire enterprise is called The Tournament of Roses Association. It is a non-profit civic organization made up of 935 members who together annually donate more than 80,000 volunteer hours to produce the Rose Parade and Rose Bowl Game, and it is supported by a 21-member paid staff whose offices are located at the Tournament House. 71 % of the Tournament members are men; 29% are women. 78% are Caucasian, 9% are African-American, 7% Latino, and 4% Asian. An effort to increase leadership diversity was undertaken as an initiative in 1994, and the amount of diversity within the membership is increasing gradually from year to year.

The Rose Bowl Game funding is derived from television revenues, interest, sponsorships, ticket sales, program sales, and concession sales. The Tournament of Roses funding comes from events, sponsorships, licensing, membership dues, entry fees, and special programs. Game proceeds pay for game expenses, conference payouts, Bowl Championship Series Contribution and Tournament of Roses Retention. The Tournament proceeds pay for city fees and rents and operating expenses.

Members of the Association serve on one of 32 committees and, in the course of their committee assignments, enjoy a wide variety of experiences as part of their membership. A volunteer member, identifiable as a *White Suiter* on Parade Day, might inspect floats at construction sites, select marching bands, work as a parade float liaison, staff a barricade, serve as a liaison to a television network, or help entertain visiting college athletes.

Committee meetings take place on weekday afternoons, usually at the Tournament House in Pasadena. Depending on the scope of a committee's function, weekend, evening, or holiday hours are sometimes required. (For information about applying for membership, see the sidebar on this page.)

The Tournament's creation of the Student Ambassador Program has given me great personal satisfaction. This program allows local high school students to volunteer with the Tournament, getting involved early in all aspects of the organization. They act as hosts to visiting dignitaries, participate in many civic functions, and help with decorating places and Post Parade activities.. It is important to keep bringing new ideas and new energy to the Tournament. I hope that they will join as volunteer members of the Tournament when they reach the age of 21.

The Pasadena Tournament of Roses, in keeping with its passion for perfection, publishes a manual for float builders. Rules, regulations, and policies concerned with float entry, design, construction,

BECOME A WHITE SUITER!

Applications for volunteer membership in the Tournament of Roses Association are available from the Association's headquarters, Tournament House, at 391 South Orange Boulevard, Pasadena, California 91184 or may be requested by calling (626) 449-4100. Weekday office hours are 8:30 a.m. to 5:30 p.m.

To be eligible for membership in the Tournament of Roses Association, applicants must:

- be at least 21 years of age,
- live or work within a 15-mile radius of Pasadena City Hall,
- devote a minimum of 30 volunteer hours on an annual basis, and complete an application and be interviewed by other members.

Once selected, new members are asked to

- purchase the official volunteer uniform, a regulation White Suit,
- attend a new member orientation, held each spring, and
- pay annual membership dues, currently $45 per year.

The membership application and two letters of personal reference must be completed and returned to the Tournament of Roses by March 1 in order to be considered for that year's class of new members, though membership applications are accepted all year.

VOLUNTEER MEMORIES

I first became involved with the Pasadena Tournament of Roses in 1989. I was a volunteer helping to decorate the City of Duarte and Kiwanis floats. While these efforts resulted in denim jeans covered in glue and flower petals, it was my first experience with the Rose Parade, and I knew then that I loved it.

As a member of a high school marching band in Southern California, it was repeatedly mentioned how incredible an experience it is to be a part of the Rose Parade, and our band tried extra hard whenever a judging panel from the Tournament of Roses was present at a competition. The year after I graduated, my high school was invited for the first time to participate in the Rose Parade. That first quarter in college was made extra special as I was asked to come back and join my high school's marching band and participate in the 1993 Rose Parade. Needless to say, it was an exhausting and exhilarating experience.

At age 24 I joined the Tournament of Roses. I was assigned to the Formation Committee and couldn't wait for the 2001 Rose Parade. In an amazing twist of fate, my high school marching band was back for its second appearance in the Parade! Once I heard this news, I mailed a letter to the committee chairman, requesting a position on the corner of Pasadena Avenue and Del Mar. That year's Parade was a fantastic experience, as I was able to meet my high school's band and spoke to all 250 students about the Tournament of Roses and the Rose Parade. Those students had a successful parade, and started their first Rose Parade experience knowing that they, too, could one day be wearing a white suit and red tie, watching their high school participate in the greatest parade in the world.

—Jeremy Dillard, CPA

judging, and post-parade viewing are presented for the purposes of safety, parade reliability, and producing the most entertaining parade possible. Any variance to the standards specified in the manual must be approved by the Design Variance Committee. (See sidebar at left for address.)

Upon receipt of a letter of interest to put a float in the Parade, the Association replies with detailed information and an application to participate. The Float Entries Committee reviews all float participant applications and makes recommendations to the Executive Committee regarding possible invitations. Invitations are then sent to those applicants approved by the Executive Committee. Acceptance is required within 30 days. As additional openings occur, additional invitations may be issued to applicants.

Float participants must include full payment of an entry fee with their Acceptance of Invitation. Self-built non-commercial entrants pay $1,800; non-commercial charitable entries pay $2,800. Non-commercial entries by countries, states, municipalities, visitor bureaus, and civic-promoting bodies as well as professional, trade, or cooperative associations pay $3,700. Commercial entrants pay $6,250.

When an organization accepts, participants may request a float builders' roster, and float builders are notified when a participant has been invited. Thus participants and builders are able to negotiate designs and other details fairly and independently. Builders who wish to be listed on the roster must contact the Association prior to January 15 if they did not build a float the previous year. The Association does not sponsor, endorse, or recommend float builders or designers, nor does it have any ownership or interest in any of those companies. Builders and designers are not allowed to be members of the Association.

Once they have accepted the Association's invitation, parade participants are assigned to members of the Float Entries Committee. Each member of that committee is assigned to a specific float. It is his or her responsibility to work with float builders and sponsor to assist them with conformance to float construction requirements leading up to the delivery of a safe and reliable float to the Formation Area during the night preceding the Parade.

The Parade Operations Committee also assigns a liaison to each float to assist builders, drivers, observers, and float riders with their performance during the actual parade. A maximum of ten persons, other than the float operators, are allowed on a float. Riders must be at least 12 years of age, and must be costumed appropriately. All floats with riders must be able to demonstrate a 45-second evacuation plan. Each builder must provide a float repair vehicle, with one or more mechanics, to be available for service in the Formation Area the night before the Parade.

Organizations interested in sponsoring a float are encouraged to write a letter to:
   Float Entries Committee Chair
   391 S. Orange Grove Boulevard
   Pasadena, CA 91184

A volunteer glues a flower to the side of a float.

A young volunteer snips petals from a flower to prepare them for application on a float's surface.

PHYLLIS M. HIX
FIRST FEMALE MEMBER OF THE TOURNAMENT

Although I am now an honorary member of the Tournament of Roses, for almost 30 years I served as the first female regular member, the first female White Suiter, a distinction that was carried out with a great deal of energy and pride throughout those years. You have asked for experiences and memories. There are many.

At the beginning, I did not realize the Tournament was all male, so naively began to obtain an application to try to submit it. That arduous process took, as I recall, about three years. Finally, two extremely fine gentlemen and courageous members, Walter Hoefflin, Sr., and William Johnstone, signed my application. During all of this process, I had become familiar with the fact that perhaps my seeking admission was not a politic thing to do. However, the Tournament was then and still is the happiest, most wholesome, family-oriented activity I have ever been exposed to. As such, the effort seemed worthwhile, and was. And, it made me determined to be the best White Suiter that I could possible be.

Being the first female regular member was not what my goal was, nor was it more than a brief blip in the back of my mind. It brought, however, the natural consequence of one person who has taken on a task not allowed to their kind before, who did it well, without any attitude except that of joy and of privilege, who was honest and truthful in their approach and who was willing to give more than they asked. Now there are numerous women members, many serving as Committee Chairs and on the Executive Committee.

My greatest thrills? Leading the parade with the United States Marshal's Possee, on J. R., now gone, and bringing up the rear of the parade on J. R. with millions of teeming people closing in on us like quicksand — a never to be forgotten and fearful experience.

And, being the person in the book and video made about it, who is credited with "the idea" for bringing the 20 Mule Team out of our wonderful past and down Colorado Boulevard, live. Being she who drew together the corporate people from here and abroad, the expert mule skinner and Tournament folk to make it a reality. Being she who, with her daughter and Past President Dick Ratliff, President of the 1999 Rose Parade, "Echoes of the Century" and his family, having the honor and excitement of being the first to ride on the giant Borax wagon in the Mojave Desert the very first time to 20 Mule Team put together for the parade was hitched to the wagons.

Among the tasks that were assigned to me and carried out by me, often with hilarity, fun, lots of good companionship, laughter, and creation of friendships, was to climb to the top of Tournament House on ladder and chairs and erect the Christmas tree; to stand all night (without relief) through freezing rain, sleet, cold, on both the busiest corners and the most forlorn corners; to serve as "secretary" to virtually every committee I was assigned to; to assist in the delivery of a baby who was determined to be born on the Tournament lawn and did not wait for the whole process before the paramedics arrived; to volunteer for virtually any need that was expressed; and to smile throughout. One time an equestrian's horse began to go out of control, the rider panicked as did the horse, aid the hysterical crying lady's dismount, then deal with the horse and woman while I sent for the Mounted Sheriff's unit to escort them to their rig.

Or, after I moved to Kern County, having my pilot fly me in all kinds of weather and fog, to Burbank, or wherever we could land, to catch a taxi whether to my Committee meeting or work assignment, then rush to fly back before dark as our local airport where I now reside as no lights!

For several years after I became a member, we had no hired security. Our instructions were "smile, but handle it." "Be firm, but smile." During those days we had only the Pasadena Police Department and a few volunteer outside law enforcement and California Highway Patrol people. We were the gentle but firm, extremely effective, law enforcement corps. We are now replaced by legions of paid people, and this is probably one of the most significant changes that stick out in my mind.

Although it was not to be during my time as an active member, to be named either to the Executive Committee or as a Chairperson of a committee, I served as vice chairman or secretary, I believe, on every committee to which I was appointed, hopefully with aplomb, energy, and competency. In addition, it was my greatest pleasure to serve as "Party Lady" to arrange two years of the grand party for the Equestrian Committee. That was extremely rewarding and just plain fun, since I ride horses and mules and have ridden in the Parade. I brought truckloads of my own silver saddles, tack gear, Indian baskets, ranch memorabilia and items and used them to supplement the wagons and other large pieces that we rented from a prop shop. Then, on another occasion, I was given the task of arranging the dinner for the coaching staffs of the visiting teams in the Rose Bowl Press Box. I brought my own entertainer, a musician, and his piano, arranged the function, and I believe that year was probably the high point for that type of party, at least from the letter that I still receive telling me about it.

I was honored to serve as a Director of the Foundation. Again, probably because I certainly am not politically correct in the eyes of most, I was dubbed the "conscience" by members of that board and other boards I served on. I was privileged to serve with wonderful people for a worthwhile cause. We accomplished a lot in the early days of the Foundation. That, too, was a high point. Friends were made and relationships were created that will be with me forever.

What else do I remember? The times before we had all of the excellent communication, Hondas and transportation, back when we would run up and down the street all night carrying messages and items. Try that in white heels and skirt! It was time well spent. The enjoyment seen on the faces of the people participating or viewing the New Year's festivities in Pasadena is awesome, not to be forgotten, never to be changed.

The commentary for the parade seen by millions of television viewers may be prepared in advance, but it is so peacefully given and in straightforward language that it educates millions of us on the goodness and purpose of so many acts of individual and group kindnesses that go on quietly throughout the year, but never come to light, the sacrifices and contributions of self by so many for the good of us all.

I am very proud to have served in my capacity with the Tournament because I believe that with the energy, enthusiasm, and always a smiling face, I helped to pave the way for other females, many of whom have now served in executive capacities with the Tournament and done it well. I am proud of that history and of the Tournament.

—Phyllis M. Hix, Attorney at Law
Kernville, California

There are no whited suited women pictured in this 1970 photo of parade volunteers because until Phyllis Hix was accepted into their ranks, there were no women to have been granted that honor.

The "Rejoice" banner goes up on New Year's Day at my mom and dad's home. It usually hangs over the garage, the colorful letters on a white background reminding the neighbors to rejoice. Something of an historical artifact, it made its first appearance on January 1, 1983, carried by two Boy Scouts down Colorado Boulevard before a million people in Pasadena in that year's Rose Parade — what we always refer to as "Dad's Parade."

That was when Dad was the President of the Tournament of Roses, the volunteer organization that runs the Rose Parade and the Rose Bowl. He and Mom traveled across the country, meeting the bands that would march in the Parade and the civic groups that would sponsor floats. They ate at pancake breakfast fundraisers, shook hands with mayors and boosters, marched in other parades, and cheered through Pac Ten/Big Ten football games. In preparation, Dad crowned a Rose Queen and selected a Grand Marshal. But his biggest challenge was to come up with a theme for the Parade.

I can remember some of the rejects: "Faith and Family," "Faith, Hope and Love," "Faith and Enterprise" (somehow I could never see that on a banner carried down Colorado Boulevard!). Clearly Dad was trying to find the right message to help people celebrate the New Year. "It should have meaning for everybody," he said.

What Dad finally settled on was a simple verb, one that appears a couple of hundred times in the Bible. It was on the banner and the floats and in the band music, and it was the word he repeated that sunny morning as he waved from the horse-drawn, flower-covered carriage that led the parade.

"Rejoice."

What a way to greet the New Year!
Rick Hamlin
from *Guideposts*

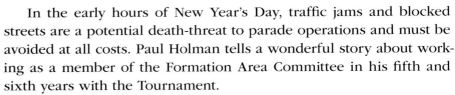

In the early hours of New Year's Day, traffic jams and blocked streets are a potential death-threat to parade operations and must be avoided at all costs. Paul Holman tells a wonderful story about working as a member of the Formation Area Committee in his fifth and sixth years with the Tournament.

"My first assignment on New Year's Eve was at a barricade on Orange Grove Boulevard. This barricade controlled vehicle access to the front driveway to Tournament House. The chairman gave me simple instructions, He showed me a credential and said, "Don't let any vehicle through this barricade unless they have this credential." As if it wasn't already completely clear, he said: "This is the only credential that gets through this barricade, OK?"

"Yessir," I replied eagerly.

Several hours passed with very little activity. As evening approached, the number of cars requesting access to the driveway increased. Each time I said "no" a passionate explanation followed as to why they must get through my barricade to Tournament House.

Gradually wearing down, and in the face of a particularly persuasive explanation, I finally let one vehicle through the barricade without the proper pass. After what seemed like only seconds had passed, my chairman rushed up to me and said, "Holman! Didn't you understand my instructions?" Thoroughly embarrassed, I repeated the excuse I had been given (which, now, seems much less persuasive) and my chairman, with a look of total exasperation, asked, "Did they have this credential?"

I meekly said, "No, Sir,"

"Then, darn it, Holman, **don't let them in! Do I make myself perfectly clear**?"

"Yes, Sir," I said.

White Suiters have heard many stories from the public trying for access to secured Tournament areas.

With this perfectly clear understanding of my mission and a new level of commitment borne of guilt and resolve not to let my chairman down again, I turned away one car after another, ignoring the passionate pleas of people who knew perfectly well that they were not credential-worthy. After a few hours had passed, a gleaming black, chauffeur-driven limousine appeared. The woman in the back seat rolled down the window and said, "Young man, unfortunately, I think I left my credential at home. I'm the mayor of Pasadena and I really do need to get to the Tournament House."

Always quick and clever with words, and thinking this was yet another creative excuse, I cleverly responded, "Of course you are; and I'm a Good-Humor Man (ice cream), and without a credential I can't let you through this barricade."

After what seemed like just a few seconds, out of breath and red-faced, my chairman stormed up to me, shouting, **"Holman, for god's sake! Have you no judgment at all? That was the Mayor of Pasadena! Why the hell didn't you let her in?"**

Brooks Vinson tells another story about being posted at a traffic barricade on Green Street early in the morning of New Year's Day in the mid-1970s. His job at that location was to keep the street clear of all moving vehicles. Out of the darkness, he was approached by an extremely large vehicle in the distance. As Brooks squinted to make out its shape, a motorcycle officer pulled up beside him, staring in the same direction. They were being approached by a huge elephant with a lovely woman, in costume, on its shoulders. There was no such entry scheduled in the parade! The elephant headed for the officer and stretched its trunk out toward him as he reported to his supervisor over the microphone: "You won't believe this, but I'm about to be removed from my motorcycle by an elephant." The supervisor chuckled and replied, "I hope it's not a pink elephant!" The officer looked at Vinson, wondering what to do.

Vinson called up to the costumed rider, "Sorry, Ma'am. No vehicles allowed on this street until the parade's over."

The woman laughed and replied than her elephant wasn't exactly a vehicle, and then steered it away, back down the street. She and her elephant had been hired to drop into a private New Year's Eve party nearby, and she had decided to investigate the parade activity on her way home.

The new Tournament theme is announced on the third Thursday of January. On the second Wednesday of February each year, a Theme/Design Draft Meeting is held at the Tournament House. Float builders and self-built participants are invited. The builders register and reserve float themes and designs at this meeting, following a clearly stipulated procedure that insures fairness. The Design/Variance Committee reviews and approves all designs for all floats and

PARADE FLOATS COMPETE FOR 23 TROPHIES

Sweepstakes Trophy: Most beautiful entry

Animation Trophy: Best display of animation

Craftsman Trophy: Outstanding showmanship and dramatic impact over 55 feet in length

Crown City Innovation Trophy: Best use of imagination and innovation to advance the art of float design

Directors' Trophy: Outstanding artistic merit in design and floral presentation

Extraordinaire Trophy: Most spectacular entry including floats that cannot retract to 55 feet in length

Fantasy Trophy: Best display of fantasy and imagination

Founders' Trophy: Most beautiful entry built and decorated by volunteers from the sponsoring community or organization

Governor's Trophy: Best depiction of life in California

Grand Marshal's Trophy: Most creative concept and design

Bob Hope Humor Trophy: Most comical and amusing

International Trophy: Most beautiful entry from outside the United States

Isabella Coleman Trophy: Best presentation of color and color harmony

Judges' Special Trophy: Outstanding showmanship and dramatic impact

Lathrop K. Leishman Trophy: Most beautiful entry from a non-commercial sponsor

Mayor's Trophy: Most outstanding city entry

National Trophy: Best depiction of life in the United States

Past Presidents' Trophy: Most innovative use of both floral and non-floral materials

President's Trophy: Most effective use and presentation of flowers

Princesses' Trophy: Most beautiful entry under 35 feet in length

Queen's Trophy: Best use of roses

Theme Trophy: Best presentation of the Rose Parade theme

Tournament Special Trophy: Exceptional merit in multiple classifications

Tournament Volunteers' Trophy: Best floral design of Parade theme under 35 feet in length

reviews theme relevance, design concept, safety, and variances. This committee screens all preliminary and final renderings to prevent duplication and check for adherence to Tournament requirements.

Prior to the Parade three judges examine each float three times: twice at the building site on the two days preceding the parade, and once at 3:00 a.m. on parade day. As is true for all of the Tournament processes, the adjudication process is spelled out in clear detail and timed carefully. The trophy winners are preceded in the Parade by a banner carried by members of the Tournament Troup, Eagle Boy Scouts and Gold Award Girl Scouts.

At the end of Parade the Post Parade Committee coordinates the display of floats for the public to enjoy.

All float participants are presented a 16" x 20" color photograph of their entry, framed in a distinctive gold-leafed Tournament trophy frame.

Between Christmas and New Year's every year, throngs of visitors and participants enter the City of Pasadena and its environs. All of their needs must be met by the city's public services and facilities. Traffic must be channeled, safety enforced, nourishment and shelter provided, health and hygienic standards maintained — all without visible effort or discomfiture.

No taxpayer dollars subsidize the Tournament of Roses events. The Tournament of Roses Association, from the very beginning, has operated on its commitment to giving back to the community, and is the only festival of its kind which is completely self-supporting and then shares its revenues with its host city. Economic impact studies estimate that the New Year activities provide an annual benefit of more that 200 million dollars to Pasadena area businesses, including hotels, restaurants, and retail stores.

In 1983 the Association created the Tournament of Roses Foundation, governed by a Foundation Board. Since its inception, the Foundation has awarded more than $1.5 million, to help support new and ongoing efforts to improve the quality of life for children and adults in the greater Pasadena area. In 2004, each team/conference participating in the 2005 game received $14,399,891.12. As Dave Davis put it, "The Grandaddy of Them All" gives out more than just quarters.

VOLUNTEERS ARE A THIRSTY BUNCH

The Tournament of Roses volunteers, staff, and parade/event participants go through 20 pallets of Sparkletts water every year during a three-day span of events. Here are some interesting facts about just how much water that is, that gets guzzled down by thirsty people involved with the Tournament of Roses:

· 20 pallets of Sparkletts, which is 28,800 bottles

· 20 pallets fill up one full load in a semi trailer

· 28,800 bottles is 14,400 liters

· 14,400 liters is 3,804 gallons

· 3,804 gallons is more than three fire truck tankers can carry when full

· It would take one average person over 7,608 days to drink that amount of water, which is over 20 years.

—Jonathan Gesinger
Sparkletts Water

(A lot of coffee gets consumed too!)

Roses are cut and placed in water vials to keep them fresh.
The roses, vials and all, are pushed into styrofoam on the float
creating a living field of red.

Police and Fire are both great supporters of the Parade and are responsible for crowd control and public safety on Parade Day.

Below: Parade participant California Fire Fighter Association

The Pasadena Police start off the parade with their motorcycle mounted officers and end it with patrol cars that separate the crowds from the last parade entry.

A White Suiter's day begins before dawn and continues long after the parade with float viewing and Rose Bowl game duties.

CHAPTER 5

Grand Marshalls
and Antique Cars

2004 Grand Marshal, John Williams and his wife Samantha wave to parade watchers.

Grand Marshals and Antique Cars

The Grand Marshal for each parade is announced during the year prior to the parade. The Tournament President chooses the celebrity, always in keeping with the theme he or she has selected for the year. I had chosen the theme "Music, Music, Music" for 2004 because I believe that music is an art form and universal language that transcends generations, cultures, borders, and boundaries to unite people's spirits through bonds of beauty and pleasure. I think that music is one of the greatest wonders of the world, and it can stir both heart and soul. Everyone, I believe, can name a song that recalls a first love, a treasured friend, or a special moment. Consider the collective voice of a premier choir, or the precision of a well-rehearsed marching band; they generate a musical power that uplifts, transforms, and entertains.

My personal connection with music began when I was five years old. My mother purchased a gorgeous pecan 6' 2" Knabe grand piano and had it placed in a prominent spot in our living room. I was, of course, consumed with curiosity, but I was not allowed to touch this marvelous musical machine until my sixth birthday. Then the lessons began. My most remarkable piano teacher was Les Hewitt, head rally chair at UCLA. Les was the guy who invented card stunts at rallies and football games, where everyone in a grandstand has a double-sided card that, when turned in properly orchestrated rhythm, works with hundreds of other cards to spell out a huge message or create a picture mosaic for the fans across the stadium. Les would work with me at the piano

JOHN WILLIAMS

John Williams was born in New York, moved to Los Angeles with his family in 1948. He attended UCLA and The Julliard School and served in the Air Force. He composed the music and served as a music director for more than 100 films including:

Amistad
Catch Me if You Can
Close Encounters of the Third Kind
E. T. (the Extra-Terrestrial)
Harry Potter and the Chamber of Secrets
Harry Potter and the Sorcerer's Stone
Home Alone 1 and 2
Hook
The Indiana Jones Trilogy
Jaws
JFK
Jurassic Park
Minority Report
Saving Private Ryan
Schindler's List
Star Wars Episode I: The Phantom Menace
Star Wars Episode II: Attack of the Clones
The Star Wars Trilogy
Superman

He's earned 42 Oscar nominations, making him the Academy's most-nominated living person. He's won five Oscars, three British Academy Awards, and three Golden Globes; 19 Grammys, four Emmys, and numerous gold and platinum records. He was Music Director of the Boston Pops for 14 seasons; and is Boston Pops Laureate Conductor. His concert pieces include two symphonies and a cello concerto. He composed "Liberty Fanfare" for the re-dedication of the Statue of Liberty, and composed themes for various Olympic Games, including the Special Olympics.

for about an hour, and then we would take a half-hour break to talk about football, and then we'd finish it off with another half hour of music. My reward was tickets for seats directly behind the air horn at UCLA games.

While the Rose Parade's visual tradition is about flowers, there wouldn't be much of a parade without music. In fact, music has been integral to the Tournament of Roses ever since the 20-member Monrovia Town Band first marched down Colorado Boulevard way back in 1891. Their drumheads were made of animal hide, a far cry from the technologically advanced polymylar lexene heads used today. Since that first musical entry in the Rose Parade 11 decades ago, more than 1,700 marching bands and more than 200,000 individual musicians have made their way along the most famous parade route in the world.

So, at the risk of bragging more than Anne would approve, I must congratulate myself for choosing the legendary composer and conductor John Williams as the Grand Marshal for "my" parade. I consider Williams an American musical treasure, an artist of Olympic proportions. You are probably familiar with several of his musical scores: *Harry Potter, Star Wars*, the *Indiana Jones* series, and *Jaws*, for example. Like many of the original founders of the Tournament, John is originally from New York. An alumnus of UCLA, he is part of the Pac-10 tradition. He holds honorary doctorates from 19 different American universities. He has earned five Academy Awards, three British Academy Awards, three Golden Globes, four Emmy Awards, and a whopping 18 Grammy Awards. And, he has been nominated for 42 Oscars!

There's quite a ceremony that takes place when the Grand Marshal is announced. The identity of the person selected is kept top secret until the formal announcement. I want to share the ceremony's timeline with you to convey the degree of precision that pervades all Tournament ceremonies.

John was picked up by limousine at his home at 10:00 a.m. on September 24th, 2003, and transported to the Tournament House. Arriving at 11:00 a.m, he was met by Caryn Eaves, Director, Public Relations; William B. Flinn, Chief Operating Officer; and Anne and me. He was escorted into the Tournament House through the kitchen to the Director's Room upstairs. There he was met by Mitch Dorger, Tournament CEO, and his wife Barbara, and refreshments were served. At 11:20 a.m. he was interviewed by the Tournament's videographer. At 11:30 a.m. Anne and I escorted John downstairs to the foyer, where I introduced him to the Tournament of Roses leadership and staff. He was then escorted into a separate room for a photo session, after which he was given a few moments to relax.

John Williams

Thank you, Mike and Anne Riffey, for this great honor. The next time I conduct Tchaikovsky's *Waltz of the Flowers* I shall use this baton.

I am overwhelmed by the Pasadena welcome so far. I am delighted to accept this for three reasons. First, of course, is that this year's celebration will honor music and particularly the high school young musicians that will come from around the country to perform here. I was in a high school band myself in the beginning of untold wonders of joy that I found from music in my life. We are all very much aware of the value of arts education for our young people. All the data confirms that academic achievement can be so closely linked to the study of art for our kids.

I'm somewhat envious of people from other countries who say their kids are required to learn two languages from a very young age. We all know what the study of language does for all of our intellectual activities, and the study of music is really like learning another language. If they start young enough they can learn to read fluently and learn the metric system of music, which is another metric system of computation which we would not otherwise have. And the study of music will enrich and contribute to their lives in a spiritual way as nothing else can quite do.

We have problems at the lower levels of our music education in our country as far as support, but we'll get over that and we'll work through it. Every year I go to Tanglewood and we see our young musicians. And our kids here at the master level are the best in the world, without any exaggeration and excess chauvinism. And so despite our troubles at the beginning, we can be enormously proud of the music education in our country. Our young musicians are like our athletes. They will jump higher and go farther and play more brilliantly than the group from the last class. It's something we can be proud of.

And so my first reason and my joy in accepting this honor is that very fact that I could represent these young musicians and, symbolically, if I may presume to that, I represent their music teachers and those who mentor their interest in music. That's a great privilege.

The second reason is that this is our uniquely American New Year's Day celebration. Like all the cultures in the world we celebrate the miracle of Mother Earth's renewal, and we want to emulate that. We make promises that we want to fix things in our lives and in our society, and we do that. So New Year's Day celebrations are a big and very important thing in the mythic sense in our culture. When I think of New Year's Day and our resolve to do better, it makes me think of hope. Even the roses themselves, and to see what people do with them in their creativity with these floats. It's an outburst of artistic creativity and is something to be celebrated every year.

My third reason for being overjoyed with this privilege is simply that my family and I have wondered for the longest time whom you have to know or what influence you must have to really get a good seat for the Rose Parade and the Rose Bowl Game, and I thought this was an opportunity that I couldn't pass up!

Thank you all very much.

John Williams

At 11:45 a.m. Ross Jutsum went to the piano on the front porch of the Tournament House and began playing a variety of music from various musical traditions — familiar classical, jazz, show-tunes, folksongs, patriotic songs, contemporary music, and some of John's compositions.

At exactly 12:00 noon, I stepped out of the front door and down the front steps of the Tournament House to a lectern while Ross played the reprise from "Everything's Coming Up Roses." Included in my brief comments about Williams's credentials I dropped a few hints before I actually announced his name. At that point, six trumpeters joined Ross in playing a fanfare. Williams came out the front door and down the steps as confetti cannons showered him in celebration. I presented him with a special baton, decorated with red roses. He then delivered his acceptance speech. Next came time for publicity photographs, television interviews and radio interviews. Then we moved into the Tournament House living room for print media interviews.

Williams wrote a special arrangement of the national anthem for the 2004 Rose Bowl game, and conducted the combined bands from both universities as they played it at the start of the football game. His arrangement originally called for cannons to be fired at strategic moments during the piece, but we couldn't round up any cannons that wouldn't mark up the Bowl's playing field, so we used fireworks instead. To top it off, U. S. Air Force stealth planes flew over while the anthem was being played and a card stunt with all 93,000 attendees participating created two American flags surrounding the entire stadium. What a thrill! John has no memory of the planes' flying over — he was too intent upon the music to notice what was happening overhead. I have a videotape of that moment — my eyes fill with tears every time I watch it. General Tommy Franks, who was my special guest at the event, commented with tears in his eyes that we (the Tournament) created miracles that day, one after another. It was a very moving experience for him.

Alex Gaal reminds me that we had three astronauts as Grand Marshals in 1967. Soon afterward, two of them were lost in a take-off accident at Cape Canaveral. He remembers also that Bob Hope was Grand Marshal in 1969. Tournament President

Jimmy Stewart waves to the crowd from a 1927 Packard as Grand Marshal of the 1982 parade.

Tyge Payne asked Alex to take the limousine with a driver and bring Mr. Hope to the Kick-Off Luncheon, which was serving about 4,000 people. Alex, who had been to Mr. Hope's home on five previous occasions, recalls it as ". . . a wonderful experience with a great and caring man."

The Tournament House archives hold video clips taken from television interviews of many of the more recent Grand Marshals. Viewing them is a good way to review history.

Jimmy Stewart served as Grand Marshal in 1982. When Johnny Carson interviewed him about the Tournament, Stewart commented that he had lived in California since 1935, but had never realized that the Tournament was run almost exclusively by volunteers. "When I went to the reception," he said, "I shook hands with every one of 500 people." He was excited about riding in a beautiful 1927 Packard, and demonstrated the "windshield wiper" parade wave that he had chosen to use.

Carson also interviewed Gregory Peck prior to the 1988 parade. Peck modeled the 1930s costume that he would wear for his ride with the Rose Queen in a 1931 Bugati Royale, worth $8,100,000. The car is part of the Domino Car Classic collection, and is trimmed with teakwood and rhinocerous hide. "It'll do 135 miles per hour, and it has 300 horsepower," Peck exclaimed. He, like Jimmy Stewart, had been coached in parade waving, but decided to choose neither the "windshield wiper" or the "screwing in a lightbulb" technique; his costume inspired him to invent the "waving the straw boater" technique. Peck grew up in La Jolla; his dad used to bring the family to Pasadena on New Year's Eve, and they would head for the parade route at 6:00 a.m. in those days. He recalled that his favorite game pitted USC against Tulane in 1932. "Jerry Dalrymple was my hero, my role model." His only negative memory of the Tournament was losing his beloved dog Bud. Bud disappeared one day while the family was attending the parade, and was never found.

Danny Kaye was, in my opinion, one of the most refreshingly candid Grand Marshals. He was a survivor of quadruple bypass heart surgery when he took the office. When interviewed on the morning of the 1984 parade, he talked about the formality of the Tournament reception held on

his behalf. He got bored standing in the reception line, so he stepped out and took a tray of hors d'oeuvres from one of the servers. He then commenced walking up to guests at the reception and saying, "Would you care for an hors d'oeuvre?" He delighted in the way they would look at the tray, make a selection, and only then make eye contact with the server, gasping in surprise to discover that they had been served by none other than Danny himself. "I am as curious today as I was when I was 15," he grinned. What an example for all of us! And what a loss when he passed away only two months after his Parade.

Lee Iacocca agreed with my thinking when he was interviewed in 1985: "I am coming to have fun, and I am honored to be part of this."

Shirley Temple Black is the only Grand Marshal to have led

three Rose Parades. Her first invitation came in 1939 when she was ten years old. She describes the experience in her autobiography, *Child Star*:

President Lathrop Leishman of the Tournament of Roses Association had first pitched the deal by saying I could ride in a flower-bedecked coach, "like a modern Cinderella." He was wide of the mark until he mentioned I would also receive an ornate badge. . . . My job was to keep waving right and left, but what I really enjoyed was ducking my chin to admire the badge and smell the flowers.

When we interviewed Mrs. Black for this book, she explained further: "Being a Grand Marshal is a pleasurable experience. I have been glad to accept each time. But for me, it is not all about the honor and the ex-

GRAND MARSHAL

citement. I consider it to be an important job that must be done responsibly. The Grand Marshal warms up the crowd and sets the tone. I don't look at the entire crowd; doing so makes you dizzy. Each time I turn and wave, I find individual people to look at."

Mrs. Black loves roses — she introduced them to the American embassy in Ghana during her diplomatic tenure there from 1974 to 1976. She tended her own rosebushes for relaxation, and cautioned us interviewers that one must prune only above five-leaf stems if one desires new blossoms. She learned the technique from the owner of Frank's Flower Nursery in Santa Monica in the thirties. ("No cut, no new bloom," said Frank.) Unfortunately, however, she is allergic to red roses, American Beauty roses in particular. Tournament staff were horrified to discover this fact after handing her a huge

bouquet of them prior to her second tenure as Grand Marshal in 1989. She gamely accepted the bouquet, but was careful to hold the blossoms away from her skin. In that parade she rode in a beautifully decorated carriage along with her daughter Susan and granddaughter Teresa. Mr. Black walked alongside, as Shirley's father had in 1939. He spoke of Shirley with great love and pride: "If the Good Lord gave me another crack at life, I'd marry her again."

Mrs. Black's third ride as Grand Marshal was in 1999, at the turn of the century. This time she rode on a beautiful float decorated with cream-colored flowers from the Netherlands. The float was built over the chassis of a truck, and the fumes from the truck enveloped the Grand Marshal, as well as Mr. Black and the two Pasadena Highway Patrol officers who strode beside the float.

"It was awful," she recalled during our interview, and then hastened to add, "but I don't think that should go in your book, because I don't want to do anything to detract from the wonderful tradition of the Tournament."

Senator John Glenn's interview for the 1990 parade was serious. The theme that year was "A World of Harmony." "We may be at a watershed in history," Glenn commented. "We may start playing a new role in world harmony for the future. The rapidity with which things have been changing has been astounding." Glenn saw the world's greatest obstacles as "enmity and opposition between communism and democracy."

Grand Marshal Bob Newhart was torn between the "queen wave" and the "windshield wiper" wave in 1991. He remarked that being in Pasadena on New Year's Day was a "singular honor" for one who had grown up in Chi-

Shirley Temple Black is the only person to have been honored as Grand Marshal three times. At left, the child star rides atop a specially made float in 1939. Right, Mrs. Black accepts the honor in 1989 in front of a poster of herself as the 1939 Grand Marshal. Far right, she was Grand Marshal once more in 1999.

Surely one of the most unusual Grand Marshal's, Kermit addresses well-wishers in 1996.

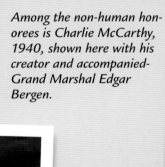

Senator, and former astronaut John Glenn accepts the Grand Marshal's job in 1990.

The much beloved Bob Hope rode as Grand Marshal twice, in 1947 and in 1969.

Among the non-human honorees is Charlie McCarthy, 1940, shown here with his creator and accompanied-Grand Marshal Edgar Bergen.

Über-businessman Lee Iococca served the Tournament in 1985.

Angela Lansbury, TV actress and Broadway legend, received the honor in 1993.

Rose Parade
GRAND MARSHAL

Pele in the 1987 Parade entitled "A World of Wonders".

"America's Sweetheart," Mary Pickford will ever have the distinction of being the first woman named Grand Marshal in 1933.

Hank Aaron in the 1975 Parade entitled "Heritage of America".

Apollo 12 Astronauts Alan L. Bean, Charles Conrad, Jr., Richard F. Gordon, Jr. were Grand Marshals in 1970.

Comedian Carol Burnett thought being Grand Marshal was "a hoot" in 1998.

Danny Kaye hams it up in front of the band during his acceptance ceremony in 1984.

Entertainer, Bob Newhart waves to the crowd on his ride in 1991.

Tom Brokow in the 2001 Parade entitled "Fabric of America".

cago in 14 degree weather. "It will be nice not to work on New Year's Eve!" he laughed. "This year I get to go to bed at 8:30!" He planned to cheer for Notre Dame that year, explaining that he was an Irish Catholic.

The delightful Angela Lansbury was the Grand Marshal for the 1993 parade. "I am absolutely floored," she explained. "During the parade I will meet 400 million people, and they know my face!" Lansbury started her career at age 17. An actress first and foremost, she chose to move to television in 1980, and feels that she became a role model for people her age. "I am venerable . . . a survivor! The Parade has not passed me by, and I can stop and smell the roses."

William Shatner, 1994 Grand Marshal, joked with his interviewers. "It's exciting to stand around from 4 a.m. until Parade time. There are no restrooms, so you don't drink coffee." He remarked that the Four Horsemen and he played together in his youth: "I was 3rd string." Then, more seriously, he added, "It's great fun. My family is excited. This is an extraordinary honor."

1998's Grand Marshal Carol Burnett began her pre-parade interview with a Tarzan yell. "Being Grand Marshal is a thrill, trip, hoot, and I haven't even gotten in the car yet!"

Tom Brokaw was the Grand Marshal in 2001, with the theme "The Fabric of America." "The fabric of America is its people," Brokaw mused. "The Rose Parade is a quintessential celebration of this country. . . . Our country is greater than the sum of its parts. We are working for common goals on a common ground." He expressed hope that America would rally behind its new President. Insightful words, and ironic in hindsight now. For the first time in Tournament history, the Parade was stopped intentionally that year. The United States Army Golden Knights Paratroopers landed on the Parade route in front of the VFW float that was a salute to Bob Hope. The paratroopers saluted the float and Mr. Hope, who saluted back.

> "Being Grand Marshal is a thrill, trip, hoot, and I haven't even gotten in the car yet!"
> —Carol Burnett

Art Linkletter has watched and participated in hundreds of parades during his long and successful career, so one might suppose that being in the Rose Parade would seem an ordinary experience for him. At age 92, he still surfs and snow-skis, and he is booked two years in advance for public speaking engagements. He is soon to publish his 27th book, *How to Make the Best of the Rest of Your Life,* which focuses on aging successfully. "People are always commenting to me, 'My, how well you look!'" he quips. "When I was 30 they didn't do that to me."

Prior to serving as one of three Grand Marshals in 2003, Linkletter had been in the Rose Parade once before as a passenger on a Farmer's Insurance Company float. He found that to be an enjoyable, although fairly typical experience except for one factor. The sponsor had invited Art to have his five children ride with him that year, but the children's participation had to be cancelled at the last minute. Unruffled, the Tournament staff implemented a back-up plan and substituted children of diverse ethnicity to represent Art's "children around the world." The parade announcers, however, did not receive script revisions to reflect that these were not Mr. Linkletter's biological offspring. Along the entire length of the parade route, he heard the loudspeakers announcing the float and giving the names of his children. "This presented me as a bit like a traveling salesman," he chuckles, "and I didn't have a microphone to correct the crowd's impression. They must have thought that I was certainly diversified in my love life."

Linkletter accepted the invitation to serve as Grand Marshal of the Rose Parade in 2003 partly because it is such a huge event, and partly because the theme that year focused on children. "I have become kind of the Pied Piper for American children over the years. I *invented* children for CBS coast-to-coast radio in 1941," he asserts. Up until that time, general consensus held that children should be seen, but not heard much. Linkletter's radio show and the subsequent *Kids Say the Darndest Things* changed that notion forever. Over the course of 26 years, Linkletter interviewed 27,000 children. "They weren't whiz kids, or freaks — just kids, and they were wonderful. I remember asking a little boy about what church his family attended. 'We're either Catholics or prostitutes,' he replied. That's genuine. I love it, because I'm a family man first and foremost. I'll never forget asking another little guy, 'What would you take with you to Heaven if you could go tomorrow?' 'My mother and father,' he replied. 'I think they'd have more time for me, up there.'"

So it made sense that Linkletter would agree to serve as Grand Marshal in a parade dedicated to children. "Our family is compulsively punctual because we've spent a lifetime scheduling rehearsals and appearances and appointments and getting to them on time," he told us. "On New Year's morning, 2003, I *thought* we were ready. "What I wasn't prepared for," he added gently, "is that this was much **more than a parade**.* It had a huge emotional impact, and turned out to be one of the highlights of my life, right up there with sleeping in the Lincoln Room at the White House, being the guest of the King of Morocco, and being Nehru's guest in India. As Grand Marshal, you are hand carried, embossed, engraved, and stamped. You go to parties, and you are escorted everywhere. When I brought my 9 grandchildren and 14 great-grandchildren to some of the events, they were almost more intrigued by the police escorts with their sirens and lights than by the events themselves."

"Riding in that car with Bill Cosby and Fred Rogers," Linkletter continued, "was like surfing for two hours on a huge, breaking wave of noise and excitement. We were all in the back of this old open car, sitting up on the top with our feet on the back seat. The crowds were huge, and I remember sweeping my gaze from side to side and waving. My cheek muscles were frozen into a huge smile for the next two weeks."

Bill Cosby was interviewed at the Tournament House and asked how he felt about serving as Grand Marshal. "Anybody who has played football knows about Pasadena," he stated emphatically. "The parade starts your day. I get to be that! It's sort of like being hired to eat Jello pudding." He added that he did not plan to go out on New Year's Eve that year. "I need to stay awake. I have two other partners, and I need to look younger." About the parade theme, he remarked, "We have to have backup to help parents. Volunteers help you get through your life and behave better. To be a part of this is refreshing. We need to highlight the good that has happened. It's a wonderful, wonderful theme."

During his interview, Fred Rogers commented, "It's a beautiful day in this neighborhood! The theme this year is Children's Dreams, Wishes, and Imagination. I am glad to see that people cared enough about children to make that the theme. Children are our future. . . .

Editor's Note: Mr. Linkletter's heartfelt words also became the title of this book.

"Without a doubt, one of my fondest Tournament of Roses memories occurred when I was just 14 years old. Being a huge sports fan, to be able to meet the baseball home-run king, Grand Marshal Henry Aaron, at the Tournament House in December of 1974 was unbelievable! Tournament of Roses member Paul Gedigian was my host that day, and Paul also sponsored my membership application into the Tournament of Roses 12 years later.

Just as memorable was a somewhat similar situation that occurred during the preparations for the 2003 Parade. Serving on the TV and Radio Committee, one of my responsibilities was arranging interviews between our media outlets and Tournament dignitaries. One such interview was with Grand Marshal Fred Rogers. He was so kind, and though he was not feeling well, he graciously received those wanting to greet him. To see the look on the faces of both my young niece Susan and my sister, Pam Mooradian, as they met Mr. Rogers brought such a thrill to my heart!

The people in and around the Tournament of Roses, along with those we serve, namely the little children, are the reason why I participate, and I eagerly anticipate what lies ahead.

—Steve Hekimian
Member since 1986

We have enormous responsibility for what is brought into the living-rooms of millions of families." When asked about the sweaters he wore on his show, Rogers shared that his mom made them for him — a sweater a month! And when asked what he'd like to teach the world, he wistfully replied, "Each person has value and longs to be loved and capable of loving. If that can be incorporated in each one of us, there won't be any war anymore."

Riding with Mr. Rogers, it turned out, was an especially poignant experience. Some time into the parade Rogers, who had been standing and waving to the crowd, confided to his companions, "My stomach is hurting! I don't think I can do this any longer." Cosby encouraged him to sit down on the regular seat and stop waving, to see if he couldn't manage to stick it out. He followed the suggestion, and was able to make it to the end of the parade.

"One month later, he passed away from stomach cancer." Linkletter's voice conveys a profound sense of respect and loss. "He was one of the most remarkable people I've ever met: unassuming, frank, forth-coming, and child-like in his acceptance of and appreciation for life."

"I was amazed to learn how much the White Suiters commit to the Tournament," Linkletter comments. "It's almost a religion: a patriotic duty, like joining the Army. You start out making sandwiches or directing traffic. 30 years later, you may end up being President of the Tournament if you've demonstrated the right stuff. And the volunteers do such painstaking work, fitting thousands of tiny, wee flowers into tiny, wee holes, all with dedication, loyalty, and a smile. The Tournament is about selflessness. People come to know each other there in ways that would not ordinarily happen.

Parade officials and their families are treated like royalty and transported in style. The President of the Tournament, the Mayor of Pasadena, the Grand Marshal, and their guests of honor ride in beautiful antique cars and carriages which have been decorated with a bounty of flowers. People often ask me how the floral sprays are attached, and whether or not the owners of the vehicles worry about scratches in the finish of their valuable cars.

The answer to the latter question is, "No," and the reason for the answer is Els Hazenberg.

Els lives in the Netherlands. She is an internationally known freelance designer and instructor, and her flower arrangements have decorated festivities all over Europe and North America. She received the Floral Nobel Prize at the 2002 World Flower Council Meeting in the Netherlands.

Silent screen actress, Mary Pickford was the very first woman to serve as Grand Marshal in 1933. Note the "white" theme: white dress, flowers, carriage, matching white horses, livery, even her drivers are decked out in white top hats and tails!

*Art Linkletter, Bill Cosby, and Fred Rogers were
honored as co-Grand Marshals in 2003.*

In a two-day process the cars are carefully protected and bales of floral foam and moss are tied down.

During the decoration process some 1,500 flower stems, only about half of which are roses, are supplemented by other flowers and greenery.

Dutch native Els Hazenburg decorates the 2004 President's car as she has every year since 1978.

The finished product ready to roll.

Els' creation for the President's auto in 2005.

Els first attended the Rose Parade with a local florist friend named Bea Frambach, who had told her for years about the Pasadena event. Bea arranged for grandstand seating for them in 1977. As she watched the parade, Els explained to Bea that, in Holland, there is a time-honored tradition of flower parades, and that she (Els) had decorated many cars, although the procedure she used was very different from what she was presently observing. Els proposed that she return the following year to demonstrate the Dutch method of automobile decoration, and proceeded to get the ball rolling by introducing herself to the Tournament staff.

When she returned to the Netherlands, Els contacted the Flower Council of Holland to sponsor her as a designer and provide the flowers. The Flower Council, financed by a mandatory levy to which all sectors of the trade in Holland contribute, is an organization that promotes the sale of floricultural products on behalf of Dutch producers and wholesalers.

They agreed to sponsoring Els, and continued to do so for 15 years. She used Dutch flowers exclusively during that time period. Since 1993 she has been sponsored by FTD® and uses mainly flowers grown in the United States.

That first year, 1978, Els's husband George Hazenberg accompanied her to see the parade and help her with the arrangements. He is a commercial grower of orchids in Aalsmeer. "After that," says Els, "he never quit! He

George and Els Hazenburg stand amid Mr. Hazenburg's greenhouse orchids in Aalsmeer, the Netherlands.

still enjoys being involved." From 1978 to 1981 they worked in the open air on the lawn behind the Tournament House. Then, a few days before the 1982 Rose Parade, it began to rain. The people could tolerate a drenching, but the old cars had to be protected at all costs, so the Tournament staff decided to rent a tent. A few hours later the tent was erected. The practice has continued.

In the early years, the Hazenbergs and their team of California floral assistants decorated only three vehicles, but their assignment increased as time went on. Cars were used to carry VIPs to the Rose Bowl after the parade. That meant an extra car was needed for the Rose Queen and her Court, and when horse-drawn carriages were used in the parade an extra vehicle was decorated for the President and the Grand Marshal, for no horses are allowed in the Rose Bowl. In 1989 a friend of Els's drove the pace car, and asked to have it decorated with a few flowers. Then the sound car was added to the parade, and that needed flowers, too.

Since 1997 cars have not been allowed in the Bowl: the VIPs walk onto the field. But Els still decorates extra cars when the President has a large family, or when there is more than one Grand Marshal. For Lieueen and Gary Thomas's 2003 parade she decorated their Presidential vehicle, a 1967 Crown fire truck. Els tells me that the most unusual vehicle she ever decorated was the Borax wagon that the 1999 President of the Tournament chose to ride in. It was a century-old, three-part wagon that once hauled tons of powdery borax from the desert. It was pulled by 20 mules, and they got flower garlands, too.

Different antique vehicles are used every year. Els has pleasant memories of decorating for celebrities like Frank Sinatra, Shirley Temple Black, Jimmy Stewart,

Danny Kaye, John Glenn, Pélé, and even Kermit the Frog. "He was probably the most unusual Grand Marshal," she remarks. In 1980, the year that Frank Sinatra was the Grand Marshal, Els was very anxious to meet him because she was so fond of his music. She found a breeder in the Netherlands who had a bright

Another of Els' creations during the decoration process in 2004.

red rose ready to be named, and approached Mr. Sinatra to ask his permission to give it his name. Unfortunately, he declined the honor, so it was decided to name the rose "Pasadena." Els and her husband brought 20 bushes for the garden at the Tournament House. Because of rules protecting against the spread of floral disease, the bushes had to be quarantined for two years in the garden of Bill Lawson, who was manager of the Tournament at that time. The bushes eventually made their way to the Tournament House, but have since been

replaced. Els did get to meet Frank Sinatra, by the way. He came to look at the car while she was decorating it, a few days before the parade.

Els has enjoyed meeting the various car owners over the years. One owner she remembers with a wide smile is the owner of Dominos Pizza. His 1931 Bugatti carried Grand Marshal Gregory Peck in the 1988 parade. The car, only half-decorated, was displayed during Peck's appearance on the Johnny Carson Show prior to the parade. Els comments, "We ate all week free pizza."

"We always have had wonderful volunteers helping us," she adds. "Many of those have become dear friends and look forward every year to being involved with the decorations and seeing us." Some of those friends have been helping for as many as 15 to 20 years. Els is now training a third generation in one family: a mother came for the first time 20 years ago with her daughter, who later married and returned with her husband and her children, who now wield a miniature broom to clean up after the designers.

Says Els, "One job that the volunteers do is to make the signs that say who is riding in the car, like 'Mayor,' 'Grand Marshal,' and 'President.' Those signs are

made of styrofoam covered with black onion seed. The letters are done in white rice. The signs are saved every year because it is a lot of work to make them. They are touched up, and the border is done with fresh rose petals in the color of the roses used on that car. One time in December I received a message that all the signs had been eaten by rats and thrown out. My poor helpers had to put in overtime that year."

Els served as a judge for the 1984 parade, and again in 2005. Her husband George judged in 2000. "It requires good planning on my part, since I am also responsible for the decoration of the cars. I will be tying the blocks to the cars myself in advance (I want to be responsible for that), and after that I can rely on my group of designers and helpers to finish the job while I am busy judging. In a way I shall miss my work and the ambiance in and around the work tent."

Els begins designing the decorations in November of each year as soon as she receives pictures of the vehicles which will be used. She selects the most appropriate varieties and colors of flowers and greens, to match the color and style of each car. The flower list is forwarded to a wholesaler in Los Angeles. The flowers come from Holland, the United States, and Ecuador.

Els arrives in Pasadena several days prior to the parade. It takes three days to do the "prep" work: wrapping the large floral foam blocks in moss and wire, unpacking the flowers, and processing them, with wire if necessary. An extremely important part of the preparation is the tying of the wet blocks of floral foam to the cars. It needs to be done securely and safely, so as not to scratch or harm the finish in any way. The blocks rest on a bed of soft foam and are fastened to the car with electrical wire. Each vehicle is fitted with 15 to 20 blocks and about 1,500 flower stems. Usually half of those are roses, which are supplemented by gerberas, tulips, chrysanthemums, euphorbias, lilacs, and orchids, among others.

The actual decoration process takes two days. Designs follow the lines of the particular vehicle, and must not block the view of driver or passengers. Els prefers bright colors, and works with the grouping technique to show off the flower varieties and greens most effectively. At three o'clock in the afternoon on December 31st, all activities stop so that Els and her team can celebrate the Dutch New Year, which precedes ours by nine hours. The Tournament Entries Committee organizes the party for them.

"We have come to Pasadena for so many years, and we have met so many wonderful people during those years," Els writes. "We have worked with 17 different Tournament Entries Chairmen. Several of them have made it to President. We've made dear friends with whom we stay in contact during the year, and we always look forward to returning to Pasadena to be with our TOR family. I cannot think of a better way to begin the New Year."

Paul Holman tells a wonderful story about the 20-Mule Team that Els mentioned. Paul served as chair of the Parade Operations Committee when Dick Ratliff was President of the Tournament of Roses. When Dick informed Paul that he would like his "presidential vehicle to be the 20-mule team wagon, Paul sprang into action. U. S. Borax, Incorporated, the maker of "20-Mule Team Borax," had one in their museum, and they generously agreed to refurbish it to make it parade-worthy. Paul contacted Bobby Tanner, the famed mule trainer, who replied that his organization did not currently have twenty mules trained to pull wagons, but that he would be happy to train and prepare a team of mules to do this job. Paul wasn't even aware that mules needed training. "They just pull, don't they?" he thought to himself. He asked what kind of training they would need. Bobby patiently explained that they needed to learn commands and how to "jump the traces." Traces are reins, two for each mule, 40 all told.

"Being slightly compulsive (a trait shared by many fellow Tournament members)," Paul continues, "I asked Bobby if he would keep me informed of the progress of the mule training, and requested that he provide a demonstration for me when they were ready. Not that I was the least bit skeptical, mind you; I just wanted the comfort of seeing the mules do their thing. Actually, I couldn't visualize ten pairs of mules jumping over the traces. I had to see it for myself."

GRAND MARSHALLS BY YEAR

1890, 1892, 1894, 1904, 1905, 1910, 1916 Dr. Francis F. Rowland

1895 Dr. H. H. Sherk

1896, 1897 Edwin Stearns

1898, 1899 Martin H. Weight

1900, 1901, 1914 Charles Daggett

1902, 1903 C. C. Reynolds

1906 John B. Miller

1907, 1908, 1911 Dr. Ralph Skillen

1909 Walter S. Wright

1910 Dr. Francis F. Rowland & Prof. Charles F. Holder

1912 E. H. Groenendyke

1913 Leigh Guyer

1915 M. S. Pashgian

1917 Dr. C. D. Lockwoo

1918 Dr. Z. T. Malaby

1919 Frank Hunter

1920 Frank G. Hogan

1921 W. A. Boucher

1922 Harold Landreth

1923 H.L. Gianetti

1924 Col. George S. Parker

1925 Lewis H. Turner

1926 Col. L. J. Mygatt

1927 Dr. C.D. Lockwood

1928 John McDonald

1929 Marco Hellman

1930 James Rolph

1931 Gen. C. S. Farnsworth

1932 William May Garland

1933 Mary Pickford

1934 Adm. William S. Sims

1935 Harold Lloyd

1936 James V. Alfred

1937 Eugene Biscailuz

1938 Leo Carrillo

1939 Shirley Temple

1940 Edgar Bergen

1941 E. O. Nay

1942 Kay Kyser

1943 Earl Warren

The city of Boron, which lies about 125 miles north of Los Angeles, holds a "20-Mule Team Days" celebration in October of each year. Bobby Tanner agreed to bring the 20 mules and the wagon to that parade to demonstrate their training. The parade administrators laid out a special "simulated Rose Parade corner" similar to the dimensions of the turn from Orange Grove onto Colorado in Pasadena.

A large and curious crowd gathered to see the demonstration. Paul positioned himself right at the corner, about 250 yards from the start of the parade. Bobby had positioned wranglers on horseback at either side of the lead mule team, "just to help them along." The whip cracked over the heads of the ten pairs of mules, and the mule train driver shouted "GEE." "That means "GO" in mulese," Paul instructs; "that's the opposite of "HAW," which means STOP."

The mules obediently leaned into their harnesses, and the 20-mule team and wagon moved forward, rapidly gaining momentum. As the mules approached the turn, the driver hauled back on the reins on the right side for the lead mules. The left-hand wrangler turned in to the left-hand mule, gently urging a turn to the right. Simultaneously, the right-hand wrangler grabbed the reins and halter at the head of the right-hand lead mule and pulled to the right.

Suddenly the expressions on the faces of the two wranglers and the driver changed from determined confidence to abject fear. The mules hadn't gotten the message! They were headed unswervingly straight for the corner — and the scores of people gathered to watch the demonstration. Paul stood

there in shock, visualizing this at the Rose Parade, and then realized that all twenty mules, two mounted wranglers, and a very large ore wagon were coming straight at him! He stood frozen in time and place. The whip cracked again. The driver commanded "HAW!" The wranglers, who apparently did not speak mulese, shouted, "Whoa, damn it!" and hauled back on the reins from both sides of the mules' heads, leaning far back in the saddle with their horses' at a stop, their metal shoes sliding on the pavement in resistance to the mules' forward motion.

The whole team finally stopped about ten feet from the end of the corner and the people gathered there. Shaken, Paul walked along the length of the train to the wagon. Before he could say a word, Bobby said simply, "Don't worry. We'll get it right at the Parade."

Paul did worry, but Dick and the Ratliff family rode happily down the parade route in their 20-mule team wagon, turning the corner, mules effortlessly jumping the traces as though they were born to do so. "Bobby Tanner," says Paul, "just smiled."

Roy Adcock, owner of Adcock Auto Supply in Riverside, California, has driven his beautifully restored maroon 1948 Lincoln Continental Cabriolet in three Rose Parades. Involved with automobiles since his youth (he owned 10 service stations and had started his auto parts business by age 35), Roy purchased the Lincoln from his wife Laura's old boyfriend (Laura scolds him when he tells this story) in Utah. Says Roy, "I got the two best things that ever came out of that valley, this redhead and that red car."

In 1995 he chauffeured Grand Marshal Juan "Chi Chi" Rodriguez, the professional golf star, P. G. A. Hall-of-Famer, and well-known philanthropist. Roy beams with pride when he describes the Lincoln as his "trouble-free car." That's a crucial attribute when one is driving a five-and-a-half-mile route at two miles per hour. Dave Cole, Editor in Chief of *The Way of the Zephyr,* a bi-monthly publication of the Lincoln-Zephyr Owners Club, emphasized this point an article for the January-February issue of 1995:

> "Among the select group of cognoscenti, there must have been several thousand [parade watchers] who could recognize the year models of each car, even though half of each one was buried in flowers and greenery, and there were probably several hundred who saw that gorgeous Continental purr around the corner from Orange Grove onto Colorado Boulevard and head east, and wondered just how far it would get before it overheated, blew its coolant all over the pavement, and had to be towed to the end of the parade."

One of only 452 manufactured (at the cost of $4,746 new), the car had been restored when Roy bought it, but he was dissatisfied with the restoration and dismantled the car again, completing his own restoration in 1994. He was very pleased with the final result, and

The 20-Mule Team Ore Wagon carried Tournament president Dick E. Ratliff in 1999.

Grand Marshals (continued)

1965 Arnold Palmer

1966 Walt Disney

1967 Thanat Khoman

1968 Everett Dirksen

1969 Bob Hope

1970 Apollo 12 Astronauts: Alan L. Bean, Charles Conrad, Jr., Richard F. Gordon, Jr.

1971 Rev. Billy Graham

1972 Lawrence Welk

1973 John Wayne

1974 Charles M. Schulz

1975 Henry L. "Hank" Aaron

1976 Kate Smith

1977 Roy Rogers & Dale Evans

1978 Gerald R. Ford

1979 Lathrop K. Leishman

1980 Frank Sinatra

1981 Lorne Greene

1982 Jimmy Stewart

1983 Merlin Olsen

1984 Danny Kaye

1985 Lee A. Iacocca

1986 Erma Bombeck

1987 Pélé

1988 Gregory Peck

1989 Shirley Temple Black

1990 Senator John Glenn

1991 Bob Newhart

1992 His Grace, Cristobol Colon & Congressman Ben Nighthorse Campbell

1993 Angela Lansbury

1994 William Shatner

1995 Juan "Chi Chi" Rodriguez

1996 Kermit the Frog

1997 Carl Lewis & Shannon Miller

1998 Carol Burnett

1999 Buzz Aldrin, Shirley Temple Black, Jackie Robinson (posthumously), David L. Wolper

2000 Roy E. Disney

2001 Tom Brokaw

2002 Regis Philbin

2003 Bill Cosby, Art Linkletter, Fred Rogers

2004 John Williams

2005 Mickey Mouse

2006 Sandra Day O'Connor

decided to offer it for use in the 1995 Rose Parade.

Now, you need to understand that the Tournament receives a multitude of offers each year from owners of vintage motor cars, and only three or four are usually chosen. But Roy went ahead and sent a letter with some photographs of his car to the Tournament officials. He was informed that he would need to haul his car from Riverside to Pasadena for road tests several weeks prior to the parade. Parade officials needed to see whether or not the car could endure traveling several miles at such a slow speed. He complied with the request and put the car through the required paces. In about a week

he received a telephone call accepting his offer and notifying him that his passenger would be the Grand Marshal, Chi Chi Rodriguez, along with Rodriguez's wife and daughter. The selection of Roy's car followed a precedent set in 1948, when General Omar N. Bradley rode in a brand new Lincoln Continental Cabriolet. A 16 year-old girl who attended that parade and snapped a photograph of Bradley's car later married Dave Cole, the author of the article quoted above, and was reminded of her snapshot when she saw Roy's car in the 1995 parade.

Roy tells me that he and Chi Chi had a great time on that ride: "Just driving in this   thing,

you feel like the Grand Marshal yourself." Chi Chi stood up much of the time, waving his golf club to the crowds as if it were a sword, and then jamming it down his side as if there were a scabbard attached to his hip. Roy seldom had to touch the accelerator — the car would just idle along — but he worked the clutch pedal to let the car coast. The crowd loved Rodriguez and cheered enthusiastically. At one point, a little five year-old boy broke away from his family and came running over to the car. He stopped and assumed a golf stance as if to hit a golf ball. Chi Chi grinned at him and commented, "You gotta keep your head down, son!" Chi Chi's daughter was amazed at

Mickey appeared in the Parade many times and accompanied the Grand Marshal's vehicle twice before, in 1966 with Walt Disney, and 2000 with Walt's brother, Roy. In 2005 he was the Grand Marshall.

Grand Marshal General Omar Bradley rides in a brand new 1948 Lincoln Continental Cabriolet.

the crowd's response to her dad. She commented to Roy, "I didn't know my father was so popular!"

The Cabriolet was used again in 1996 and 1997. As far as we know, it is the only car to be used three times in succession to escort Rose Parade grand marshals. The 1996 passenger was the first non-human Grand Marshal to lead the parade all by himself: Kermit the Frog. The 1997 co-Grand Marshals were Olympian champions Shannon Miller and Carl Lewis.

Caryn Eaves, a Tournament staff member, recalls Steve Wittmeier's expertise with the muppet. "No one looked at Steve when we talked to Kermit, even though Steve was standing right there! The frog was so animated that we all focused on it and talked to it ourselves." Kermit the Frog was to perch on the back of Roy's car on the canvas top of a unique compartment that had been constructed to accommodate Steve and two viewing monitors that would allow Steve to see the crowds and their reactions to Kermit. Getting Steve installed in the car was no easy situation; he is over six feet tall, and he had to share the compartment with those monitors, some speakers, and a microphone, keeping himself absolutely hidden so that children along the route would not be disillusioned. He gamely folded himself up into the compartment, commenting, "All I need is a pillow and a jug of water." Steve animated Kermit by manipulating sticks through a hole in the compartment cover, speaking Kermit's voice into the mike and making him wave and gesture and smile and nod to the crowd. Things went beautifully until, a few blocks from the end of the parade, Roy noticed that Kermit's ebullient personality seemed to be flagging. Roy inquired, *sotto voce*, as to Steve's welfare and state of mind. A quiet, almost desperate voice responded, inquiring about the number of blocks left to be traversed, and informing Roy that, if they couldn't get to a restroom soon, there would be dire consequences. Roy knew that they wouldn't make it to safety in time, but was able to comfort Steve with assurances that the compartment was fully lined in leather.

Later, at the Rose Bowl, the officials realized that Grand Marshal Kermit might experience a bit of trouble with the traditional flip of a coin that determines who kicks off first. Kermit graciously deferred to Mrs. Jim Henson, wife of the deceased Muppet creator.

In 2005, Mickey Mouse served as the second non-human Grand Marshal in the Parade's history. He had ridden in the Grand Marshal's car once before, with Walt Disney himself. Each time, Mickey was greeted by high-pitched squeals of joy from all of the children in the stands.

CHAPTER 6
Strike Up the Band

The Londonderry Lancers marching in the 2004 parade. Inset: A fan shows off his humorous sign encouraging the marchers. Previous page, the Pasadena City College Honor Band fills the frame in a sea of red and white.

Only 5 ½ Miles To Go

Strike Up the Band

Hundreds of thousands of musicians have marched to the roses since the Monrovia Town Band became the first Rose Parade band in 1891. As many as 5,000 band members march, twirl, or dance their way down the Parade route each year. International bands come from Australia, England, Switzerland, Japan, Mexico, and other nations around the world. The Salvation Army Band has been part of the parade since 1920. Each year, the Parade features the Marine Corps Composite Band, the Pasadena City College Tournament of Roses Honor Band, the Los Angeles All-District Honor Band, and the two participating Rose Bowl Game University Bands.

Fifteen additional bands are selected from across the United States for positions in the Parade. To ensure that the entire country is represented, it is divided into 12 regions and one band is selected from each region. Each band should have a minimum of 150 playing members.

The preparation for New Year's Day requires much more than just music rehearsal. Bands are chosen 14 months before the actual Parade. Some highly regarded, award-winning bands, have never been in a major parade. They do not know what socks to wear to prevent blisters, or how to meet the high standards of excellence of the Rose Parade, which requires them to play virtually without interruption for the entire 2 hour and 10 minute duration of the Parade.

I have received the call four times, once for my Riverside, California, John North High School Band in 1983, and three times for the Riverside Community College "Marching Tigers" Band, the first community college band to be invited. I can even remember where I was and what I was doing when each call came in.

The highlight of highlights was being selected as the lead unit for the 1990 event. Being the first band in the first Parade of the new decade meant being on the street earlier, waiting longer, and battling with nerves and the cold. Watching the sun come up, surrounded by my band "family" was a real treat. Just about the time we felt we just couldn't wait any longer, Mike Riffey came up to say "Happy New Year!" and to encourage us to play as we stepped off.

As we turned the famous corner, with absolutely nothing in front of us but thousands of people, hundreds of reporters, and dozens of television cameras, I was overwhelmed with emotion. The crowd roared with excitement — after all, they had been waiting, too! When our musical and visual presentation met their collective energy, the resulting wave of appreciation swept us down the street. "Go, Riverside!" "You're looking good, Riverside!" they shouted, for the next two hours.

It's not a parade. It's a flower-filled love-fest, played out for the entire world to see. And that's why it is the most coveted invitation a marching band can receive. It costs money; it takes time — hours and hours of preparation; it demands the coordination of effort, support, and practice, practice, practice. But I can't wait to do it again!
—Gary Locke, Director
Riverside Community College Band

Many of the bands have never been involved in an event that requires such extensive travel. They have never had to raise the $1,000 or so per band member needed to send their musicians to such an event. This type of financial investment requires intensive, creative fund-raising. In the past, fundraisers have ranged from raffling off a house to creating a cornfield maze using the Tournament of Roses logo.

The President of the Tournament of Roses helps in these efforts by traveling across the country to visit each band, participating in some of their fundraising events, and igniting the community spirit to help get their area bands to Pasadena.

It originated as a 1969 NBC television program called *Band Review*. It was hosted in the early years by Gary Owens, Bobby Vinton, Michael Landon, Jerry Lewis, and, finally, Doc Severinsen.

In 1980, the Music Committee of the Tournament of Roses changed *Band Review* to a modest single event field show called *Bandfest*, staged on the old Horrell Field at Pasadena City College. In 1995 Bandfest moved to the newly-created Family Festival site in the shadows of the Rose Bowl, and it was expanded to two days with three performances. In 2002 Bandfest moved back to the new Robinson Stadium at Pasadena City College.

For the 2004 Parade, Remo Belli designed special drum heads for percussion instruments that displayed both the Tournament Rose logo and the 2004 theme, "Music, Music, Music." He produced two special nine-foot diameter drum heads and mounted them on a triangular chassis that was decorated by Larry Crain and pulled by six people. I used this assembly in place of the traditional white satin theme banner, just behind eleven trumpeters who heralded the start of the Parade. On either side of the whole apparatus, a young woman and a young man carried massive mallets that they used to beat the drum in time to the music. The young woman had to leap off the ground with each beat, in order to reach the center of the drum. After the Parade was over, some Tournament pranksters deposited the whole apparatus in my front yard. My grandkids had to cover their ears when we beat the drumheads, because the reverberations were so powerful. I still have one of the mallets, together with the "Music, Music, Music" satin banner that was never used.

The Rose Parade bands face the highest challenge in the Parade, but they also earn the highest reward. The sense of achievement they feel, and the moments experienced by these young musicians are something unique. Despite blisters and early morning cold, everyone involved seems to retain only wonderful memories of the experience.

One example Brian Flynn remembers vividly is when a band from Ohio was selected to play in the Parade. We covered their story on video from the day they were chosen until the Parade. He says, "I'll never forget that, when the 17 year-old drum major turned the corner and looked down Colorado, he said it was the best thing he'd ever seen in his life. 'Blue sky, sunrise, and half a million people.'"

We don't leave anybody behind if we can avoid it. We try to find out about any students with special needs prior to the parade so that we can accommodate all instances as best we can. For example, some of the kids in the bands are diabetic, and we need to be prepared for their possible needs. We intend that every kid will have an extreme experience marching in our parade.

In 1990 a young lady from Upland High School in California was in an automobile accident

A giant drum signals the start of the 2004 Parade.

two nights before the parade and broke both legs. Her face was pretty cut up, as well, from the shattered windshield. Her director wanted to know if she could still be in the parade! I was the Music Chairman at the time, and I responded, "Absolutely, as long as someone can push her in a wheelchair and she can wear her full dress band uniform."

On the morning of the parade, the Music Committee Chairperson is the one who cues each band to join the parade at the intersection of Orange Grove and Del Mar. Before the parade began, I had time to walk back to the assembled band. There was the young lady, in full Tartan uniform, ready to go. I knelt down beside her and thanked her for coming to the parade. "It's really great to have you here today. I want you to have a great time," I told her. The Director commented several days later on how special that was for her.

Before the 1991 parade, a band director from Missouri contacted us with the concern that one of his students, a sophomore,

Upland High School band marches down Orange Grove at the beginning of the 1990 parade.

had lost his leg above the knee in an automobile accident about six months before they were invited to the Parade. The student had received a prosthetic limb, but was still getting used to it. He kept falling at practice on the football field because of the uneven surface, but was determined to make the trip to Pasadena with the other students. "His parents are coming to the Parade!" the director worried. "Is there anything we can do to help him?"

We decided at our end in the Music Committee that we would have a Honda motor scooter travel with the band the whole length of the parade, which is not usually done. We would take this fellow in and out of the parade when he got tired and allow him to march most of the way. We instructed the rider of the Honda to make sure that the young man was put back into the line of march one block in front of where his parents were sitting so that they could see their son marching by with the balance of the band. The plan worked perfectly, and the young man's parents never knew that we had taken him out of the line-up periodically to rest and then be put back in. Later, the band director's "thank-you" note indicated that we had done something very special for the whole band and this young man's family.

Andy Soucy, Band Director of the Londonderry High School Lancer Marching Band and Colorguard, has led his group in three Rose Parades. His experience conveys the incredible effort that any band and its supporters put forth in order to participate:

"We received our first invitation via telephone in late 1990 for the 1992 Parade, when Bob Cheney was President of the Tournament of Roses. Our band had already done some significant traveling, but what we were about to embark on was truly going to be a 'Voyage of Discovery' (the theme for the 1992 parade).

Letters of congratulation from our United States and state senators, along with letters from our congressman and other state representatives, together with constant media coverage, quickly confirmed that this was our most significant undertaking yet. We thought in the beginning that it was because we were the first band from New Hampshire to ever participate, but learned over time that this was standard excitement when it comes to the Tournament of Roses.

A unique fundraising success was "Pennies for Pasadena," a canister donation program. Marked containers were placed next to almost every cash register in town, allowing customers to donate any change they wished. The cans brought constant visual publicity as well as a surprising amount of cash. (We used the program again for our two return visits, later on.)

When it gets cold in New England it becomes diffi- cult to find the best time to rehearse — afternoons, evenings, weekends, weekdays. As luck would have it, however, there happened to be a closed-down department store in town at this time. We approached the corporate owners of the property, who turned out to be graciously receptive toward our request and allowed us full use of the facility. This meant we now had an indoor practice hall, and we ended up using it constantly. We even used it in the early mornings and evenings for aerobics sessions for the students. Every participant had to do an aerobics class twice a week. We set up a schedule of five classes, and every participant was required to attend at least two per week. On several occasions, members of the media would drop by, including our state ABC affiliate, to do update stories on our preparations. When January 1 arrived, the Lancers were able to present a terrific debut, and all students completed the route without a single dropout. We had put the building to good use. We used it for the last time two weeks after our return from the Parade for a celebration banquet.

In November of 1995 I received our second telephone call, inviting us back to Pasadena for the 1997 Rose Parade. Like the first time, the call was an emotional experi-

PRICELESS MEMORIES ARE MADE OF THIS

"Heads Up! Shoulders Back! Feet Together! Eyes, with PRIDE!" That is the chant that the West Des Moines Valley High School Marchmasters recite, and the command that we receive, before every performance. As we prepared to step off at the start of the 2004 Tournament of Roses Parade, our directors gave us two additional orders: "Enjoy every minute of this once-in-a-lifetime experience!" and "Remember to look down Colorado Boulevard as you round the big corner, for a sight you will never forget!"

It was at that moment that it struck me: at the ripe old age of 16, I was about to start playing my set of five tenor drums for the largest audience I would ever have. No matter where my love of drums and music might take me, I would never have another audience like this. One million people, all with their eyes glued to me and the rest of the Marchmasters! One million sets of eyes, watching my every step.

In this sea of eyes, however, there was one set that made an especially lasting impression on me. They belonged to a cute little girl who, looked to be no more than five years old, and had the most beautiful pair of brown eyes that I had ever seen. Our eyes met less than a mile from the end of the Parade route. The Parade had ground to a halt while needed repairs were being made to a float that had broken down. Out of the corner of my eye, I spotted this cute little girl in the front row, staring at my hands. She was trying to tap her fingers to the beat of my drums. I turned my head toward her, and she smiled up at me. Her eyes locked on me as I continued to march and play in place. It was as if I were the only person in the entire Parade.

At last the float problem was fixed and it was time for us to move on down the Parade route. At that moment I broke ranks from the band (for the first and last time, ever), stepped over to my new friend, and handed her one of my extra drumming mallets. She glanced at the mallet, looked back up at me, and gave me a big grin. I smiled right back and nodded my head in her direction. We didn't speak — we didn't have to. And then, as they say, the band played on.

Just being a part of the 2004 Tournament of Roses Parade was a great experience. The thrill of having my parents and friends at the Parade in Pasadena to watch me perform was an indescribably feeling. My chance one-in-a-million encounter with that cute little brown-eyed girl . . . priceless!

—Colin Smith
West Des Moines Valley High School
Marchmasters

ence. A feeling of pride and good wishes for the Lancers' upcoming adventure was on everyone's mind, as the community now understood the significance of the Rose Parade even more than before."

An inspirational story from this second Rose Parade trip centers around a young man named Brian Paciulan. As a child Brian had cancer, and as a result of a series of complications now had only one lung. Now a student in the high school band, he contemplated not participating in the Rose Parade project after learning how important physical conditioning was going to be. After some serious thought, he decided to give it a try. This young clarinet player trained and participated fully for a year, and never even complained once. On January 1, 1997, the big day had arrived and everything went off smoothly. When we reached the end of the Parade, I walked around to check on who was hurting, when I saw Brian literally crying for water and reaching for his sides. I yelled for water, which was readily available, and shouted at him repeatedly, "You did it! You did it!" At our celebration banquet that night, back at the hotel, I re-told the story to everyone present as part of my speech. At the moment I finished, everyone quickly rose to his or her feet and gave Brian a long standing ovation. It was a teary moment for everyone, and indeed a tribute he so truly deserved. In the summer of 2002, Brian had a successful heart transplant, and he continues to do well today.

The phone call for the 2004 Parade came in October of 2002. I just couldn't believe it! This one just had to be the best, so thoughts of how we could make this the "perfect" trip were constantly on my mind. For starters, we planned on making the announcement at the last home football game while the students were on the starting line for their halftime show. So when the moment arrived, we had arranged for a twenty-foot Rose Bowl "Congratulations" banner to be lowered from the scoreboard as the announcer read a prepared script. The fans cheered and shouted, cake, music, and plenty of talk of traveling to California followed.

When the Lancers first arrived in California for the Parade, all was going smoothly and according to plan. Little did we know that the students were becoming ill. By December 30th, 39 students were not able to perform in the evening Disneyland Parade because they were back at the hotel, sick to their stomachs. This had never happened to us before. When the rest of the band returned to the hotel after our performance, our medical parents had come up with a plan to deal with the illness. Students who were ill were not going back to their original rooms, but instead to a block of other rooms so that each student's medical condition could be monitored. New toothbrushes were purchased, and everyone was told not to share beverages, etc. Essentially, a MASH unit was set up, and proved to be quite successful. Students were unknowingly giving the illness to one another. Thankfully, it was a quick passing situation, approximately 24-36 hours. As this was the first time that a situation such as this has ever occurred in our traveling history, we were most fortunate to have these heroic parents on hand to take charge. On January 1, only four students remained at the hotel; all of the others were able to complete the Parade.

It was now the day of the Parade, and we were in the staging area waiting for the Parade to begin. At approximately 7:45 a.m., I couldn't believe my eyes as I looked up to see President Mike Riffey coming by to say hello to the band. "What are you doing here, Mike?" I asked. "It's almost parade time!" He had stopped over to show his appreciation to some of the performers before the start of the Parade. His gesture touched us all deeply, and reminded me of the numerous conversations I had had with other participating band directors prior to the Parade,

noting that Mike Riffey's theme, "Music, Music, Music," had done so much for the advocacy of music in our schools that year.

Tournament of Roses memories will always be a cherished part of Londonderry's history. The Tournament has brought countless families in this small New England community together to work toward a common goal. The names of Bob and Ruthie Cheney, Bill and Lynne Johnstone, and, most recently, Mike and Anne Riffey will be well known in these parts for

"The Tournament brought countless families in this small New England community together to work toward a common goal."
——Andy Soucy

a long time to come.

Several of the bands each year represent entire geographic areas, as opposed to a single school or group. The Wyoming High School All-State Marching Band is one of these. In 2003, 12 directors/staff members were hand-picked from all over the state, and then 225 students were selected from 47 high schools to make up the band. One of my favorite band stories illustrates the logistical complications in getting all of those teenagers together for practice. All of the band members were assembled for an overnight stay in the Cody

High School gymnasium. As one would predict, the students were talkative even though the hour was late. An exasperated chaperone announced, "If you want to stay up all night and make noise, we'll just go out to the field and practice!" Within moments the gym was quiet and the band members were settled down for the night.

Director Dave Bellis and his wife Dawn put together a daily diary and pictures on their Web page for the students to download. Here's their description of the sequence of events:

The day the acceptance letter was received, a single red rose was delivered to each of the staff members with no note attached. All had been anxiously awaiting word from us, and the telephone calls began to come in as the meaning of the rose sunk in. Our work had just begun.

Applications to each of the high schools in the state were sent out. In February, the selection of the band took place over a weekend, with all of the staff converging on a central location in the state.

Once the students were selected, uniforms had to be ordered for each one, music selections made, and the week-long summer camp organized. Airlines were not willing to lock in prices almost a year in advance, and students needed to commit to the band knowing what the cost would be. So, we decided to take buses to

Pasadena. Pepsi and Eckroth Music agreed to be our corporate sponsors again.

The band members brought a variety of experience when it came to marching: some had never marched because they attended a school where there were only 15 students in the band; others were from very strong marching band programs with a variety of marching styles. The goal of the directors was to merge all into a cohesive unit. This would occur during the summer, starting with a week-long camp, followed by five parades in various locations around Wyoming. Students would literally travel up to 450 miles to practice!

At the end of the summer, friendships were put on hold until the students would see each other again — in Pasadena! The following is a diary that captures the experience of the trip.

December 26, 2003

The bus trip started out with lots and lots of snow! Pickup in the northeast corner of the state was at 3:30 p.m. Six more buses were to be picked up throughout the day and night as they made their way to Provo, Utah, where they were to rendezvous. Anxiously anticipating calls from each bus were the directors in Downey, California. By the middle of the night everyone was boarded on their respective bus and all were making their way to Provo.

December 27, 2003

Finally all seven buses are ready to roll on their way to California. Movies are watched, food is shared, jokes are told, and even songs are sung. In Downey, the directors are busy changing drum heads, setting up registration, and marking the parking lots where practice will occur. As Mrs. Bellis receives phone calls, she updates the directors. Delays finally cause the directors to cancel rehearsal for the first night.

Then it happens! A call to the directors informs them that five windows have been broken in two different buses. A call to the head bus driver confirms that on two buses windows have been shot. Thankfully, the windows

The Wyoming High School All-State Marching Band marching early on their way down the parade route.

ONE PEPPERONI, TO GO PLEASE...

I can remember the initial call I received from John Fossleman, the Tournament of Roses representative for our region, asking if we would be interested in applying to participate in the 2004 Parade. I initially thought this was a hoax and began investigating this Fossleman person. This was the beginning of a two-year ride, which we are still cherishing to this day.

Little did I know how much work was really involved in getting the audition materials ready. To produce the Parade audition, I went to the Ambridge Police Department and asked them to close four blocks of the street that the high school sits on. After some pleading and begging, they made arrangements to reroute the traffic for two hours while we made our videotape. I sent the audition tape off to Pasadena. Now came the wait.

My family owns a pizza shop, where I spend some time making pizza when I am not in school, so one of the phone numbers I put on our application was the pizza shop's. Late one evening, as we were getting ready to close, the phone rang and my brother noticed the call said "California," so he told me I'd better answer. I picked up the phone, and sure enough, it was John Fossleman. He began by telling me that the Music Committee had met

and made its decisions on the bands that would be accepted to the 2004 Tournament of Roses Parade in Pasadena, California. He proceeded to tell me, in a somber voice, that they had reviewed all of our materials, and that there was a problem.

Why would they call to tell me that we were not accepted, when a Dear John letter would have been sufficient? How would I tell the students and the entire school that I appreciated all they had done to prepare the audition materials, but we were not accepted? Then I cleared my mind and asked John what the problem was.

He responded, "How are you going to get 300 students to Pasadena on January 1, 2004, for the Tournament of Roses Parade?"

I immediately called my principal, and couldn't wait to get to school the next day to make the announcement. The following day the buzz was already through the school, as my niece, who works in the pizza shop, is also in the band and had begun calling her friends as soon as she got home.

—Sal Aloe, Director
Ambridge Area High School Band

are double-paned and no one has been hurt. After a visit with the California Highway Patrol, the buses roll on to finish the last hour before arrival at the Embassy Suites in Downey.

Getting to California wasn't easy, but we were finally here and in relatively good spirits. Now the fun could begin.

December 28, 2003

A good night of sleep helped everyone have a great perspective on the day. The adult guests headed out to see the float building, while the students headed over to Downey High School for their first practice. Practice included sectionals to review routines and music, and then the band marching round and round the parking lot to get back into marching precision. Drum cases and baritone horn cases were set up to simulate 'the corner.'

The adults and guests are treated to seeing thirteen floats in various stages of preparation for the Rose Parade. Seeds, bark of trees, and lots of flower petals are being meticulously attached. Various booths and a chili cook-off outside the Rose Bowl gave plenty to view and enjoy.

Evening included some time for rest and relaxation, and then an evening practice in the dark. Finally, we had our first nightly meeting to discuss plans for the next day.

December 29, 2003

Today started out similar to yesterday. Sectionals are followed by marching practice. However, three directors and Talon (the drum major) are not at practice. They are on their way to the working meeting, to see the route, hear the final details about performing in the Parade, and then stop at the Wrigley Mansion, which is now the Tournament of Roses House. The house is decorated for Christmas and is absolutely beautiful.

December 30, 2003

Disneyland Day! After packing the buses with everything needed to perform that afternoon, we were off to a fun-filled morning and early afternoon. At the appointed time we met at Toon Town and were taken backstage to change and get ready for the afternoon parade. Sharing the dressing room and a warm-up area with two other bands of about 600 members strong is an experience all by itself. After warm-ups it is time to go to the gate and wait for our turn to enter the parade route.

As the Wyoming High School All-State Marching Band is welcomed on the Disney loudspeakers we enter to thousands of people lined along the streets. Much too quickly the parade is over and we have the rest of the day to play. As we get close to the end of the parade we get to watch the second parade with

Wyoming flag twirlers performing their routine during the parade.

three more Rose Parade bands. It is the only time we will get to see and hear them, so we stand on the sidelines and cheer them on.

It is a great experience, but we know that it is only preparation for 'the main event' — the ROSE PARADE!

December 31, 2003, New Year's Eve

The band heads to Knott's Berry Farm and then everyone meets for dinner at Medieval Times. Back at the hotel, we have our pre-parade meeting with last-minute instructions, and then decide we will celebrate New Year's on Eastern Standard Time so we can get some much-needed sleep. At exactly 9:00 p.m. (midnight in New York), we all come out of our rooms and yell "Happy New Year!" Hugs and kisses are shared as we bring in 2004, and then it is time to crash.

January 1, 2004

At 4:30 a.m. the VIPs in the group head by bus to the Rose Parade. Mr. and Mrs. Eckroth and family and Mr. and Mrs. Clay (Pepsi) and family are about to see the band they sponsor perform for the first time.

At 6:30 the band and directors, after loading equipment, head for the parade in full uniform. Ten students had been chosen to ride to the parade in style in a stretch limousine. For them, comfort and amenities are available. The rest of us are all nerves — what will it be like? Can we all make it? Will everything go okay? Did everyone remember everything to perform?

Soon it is our turn to unload. We are given seven minutes to do so, but they are running behind so we need to hurry. Hurry we do! Mr. Frazier times us and it takes 1:47 minutes to unload and we are on our way up the off-ramp to the street where we will form up. Warming up horns, straightening scarves, pit stops at the Port-a-potties, and it is time to go. Each section does its warm-up thing, and then it is our turn to turn the corner at Orange Grove Boulevard.

Oh, my gosh! There are literally walls of people! Both sides of the street are lined with massive bleachers, all looking at us. Well, this is what we prepared for, and we're going to do it right. Ahead is 'the corner.' TV cameras are everywhere with microphones sticking down from the sky. As we turn the corner, the float in front of us breaks down a bit and we are slowed way down, but then we're on our way again. Non-stop playing makes the first few blocks kind of a blur until we hear this big cheering section on our left. It is our VIP section, and they have garnered support from those sitting around them to yell for the Wyoming High School All State Marching Band. Mr. Clay has handed out Wyoming pins to all those who will yell.

Just traveling to California was a great experience for me! I would never have thought that I would be able to participate in the Rose Parade. I used to dream of being about 20 years old and traveling to watch the Parade with a few of my friends. I thought that it would be a great experience to camp out on the streets, just to be able to see the Parade on New Year's Day. I had no idea, then, that on my sixteenth birthday I would actually march in the Parade I had only dreamed of watching.

Our schedule was extremely busy. In a way, I wish that I had had a little more time just to absorb and remember every detail. I am glad of one thing that we did not do more of, though: practice! The band's schedule included amusement parks, restaurants, a dinner cruise, a Christmas play, a tour, and. my favorite, free time! Although everything was very exciting, sometimes all I truly desired was a nap.

On New Year's Eve, I watched the ball drop in New York City. I only slept about four hours. Our band had been preparing for the Parade's length for months. The Parade is extremely long, but it was so exciting because of all the people watching. As our band marched by, I could hear yelling and clapping all around us.

The Rose Parade was a once-in-a-lifetime opportunity, a wonderful experience. I will never forget certain details of the parade and the overall trip. I have plenty of pictures, memories, and a homemade videotape of the entire trip to remind me of all the exciting activities we were involved in and of all the fun that we had.

— Carrie Richardson
Carrollton, Georgia

It causes goose bumps to know they are all yelling for us!

While the students are busy marching with precision and playing "Magnificent Seven," "Ghost Riders," and "Western Medley," the directors are busy smiling, waving, shaking hands, and being proud. Soon the thought comes that Colorado Boulevard goes forever. As far ahead as you can see are people, and the street appears to meet the horizon. The White Suiters tell us to catch up with the float in front of us, so we are moving fast. Many are sure we will not be able to keep this pace up and have everyone make it through the Parade. All of a sudden a cheer begins to be heard from the crowd ahead on the right. There they are — our parents

and guests, and they are standing and pointing and waving. Smiles and tears are evident on their faces and it gives you a really warm feeling deep inside to know that they are there for us. In addition, the White Suiters now know that the float behind is broken down too, so we are able to do a stand up performance in front of our group of supporters.

Since we have no one directly in front of us and no one directly behind us, we are able to set our own pace and stop once in awhile to play for the crowd. Finally we come to the corner at the end of Colorado Boulevard, signaling that only a half mile remains. Feet are a little sore, but the crowd is so happy to have us play that we ignore the

pain and keep on entertaining.

As we turn the last corner we are still performing, knowing that the Parade is about to come to an end. We stop — silence for a moment — Mr. Bellis announces the instructors are so proud, and finally "at-ease." Hugs, tears, slaps on the back, and expressions of satisfaction and relief are evident.

After dropping off the hats and instruments on the buses, we are treated to what is surely the best hamburger in the world. Then we load the buses the trip back to the hotel.

Parents and guests greet us at the back door of the hotel with congratulations and cheering. Exhaustion takes over as we make our way to our rooms so that we

can turn on the television and watch "us" in the parade. As we appear on the screen, the screams and cheers take over the center of the hotel as students, staff, and guests make their way out on the balcony to cheer. We look GREAT! It now sinks in: WE DID IT!

Later we have a pizza party and a going-away meeting. Tears flow as the staff shares their experience and their thanks.

Finally, the last chance to share good times with new-found friends arrives. A dance from 8:00 to 11:00 provides an outlet for excess energy. Some students choose to find a quiet place to just sit and talk. Others shake it up on the dance floor. A good time is had by all. January 2, 2004

Reality hits. It is time for this fairy tale to come to an end. This group has become quite attached, and that means letting go is not easy. One by one the buses load and prepare to leave, but not without lots of hugs, tears, address exchanging, preparations for reunions, and thanks. It has been a good trip. Each life of each person involved has been changed, and the memories are there forever.

This drum major from the Los Angeles Unified School District Honor Band shows pride and confidence. Left, baton twirlers from Pasadena City College Band perform their dance and twirling routine for the crowd.

These Pasadena City College Herald Trumpets traditionally signal the beginning of the Parade or "hearld" the coming of the Queen and her Royal Court. Below, Conseruatorio de las Artes de Catago Band of Costa Rica 2005, whatever these drummers may lack in disciplined precision, they make up in sheer ENTHUSIASM!

The first ever appearance of a band from Mexico was a moment of pride for Mexicans and for the many Mexicans living in California.

Marching the Tournament of Roses Parade is a once in a lifetime experience and one young musicians cherish.

Even if marching bands are your favorite part of the parade experience, they can get LOUD!

The Marine Corps tuba players warm up before the parade.

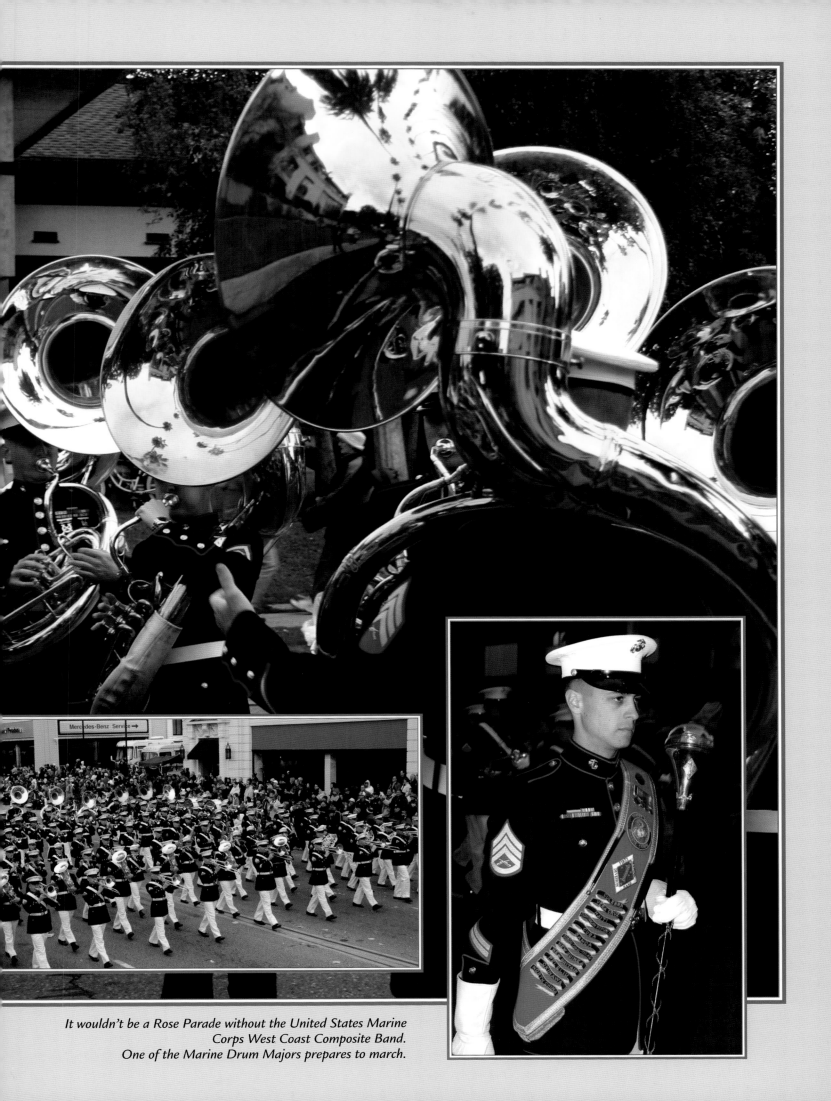

It wouldn't be a Rose Parade without the United States Marine Corps West Coast Composite Band. One of the Marine Drum Majors prepares to march.

Silver Saddles and Borium Shoes

This beautiful Arabian horse poses for a picture while he waits for his entrance onto the parade route.

Silver Saddles and Borium Shoes

One of the Tournament positions that I especially enjoyed was chairing the Equestrian Committee. Equestrians provide a connection to the Tournament's very roots. In the first parades, the residents' flower-bedecked wagons were pulled by horses. The "Never on Sunday" tradition dates back to the old days on Colorado Boulevard. The Valley Hunt Club members, all horsemen, didn't want to, as Brian Flynn puts it, "create a ruckus that would disturb the church services."

Parade wagons evolved into horse-drawn platforms, which eventually gave way to motor-driven floats. By the 1920 Tournament most floats had been motorized, but equestrian units continued in their popularity. Tournament records note that the 1915 Parade even featured an elephant with a rider, and ostrich-driven racing buggy, and a float drawn by six camels carrying lions, tigers, and leopards.

The year 1934 ushered in an Equestrian Committee requirement that all equestrian entrants must use silver-mounted trappings and riders must be outfitted in Spanish costumes. That rule was modified in 1946, however, when Western trappings became popular. Variety in trappings and costuming is celebrated now, and the Tournament strives to showcase different breeds in the Parade as well.

Equestrian applicants apply for placement before June 1 each year. The Tournament notifies the selected groups in August. Each rider must carry an insurance policy. The riders and the horses must practice thoroughly, as no one wants any accidents to happen due to an animal's skittishness or fear.

Phil Spangenberger has marshaled his group, The Spirit of the West Riders, in the Rose Parade every year since 1992. His group rides on behalf of the John Wayne Cancer Institute. He and his rough riders have helped many charities, and have produced and performed in numerous programs to benefit handicapped children and wildlife organizations. A Field Editor for *Guns & Ammo* magazine for over 33 years, Spangenberger now writes a column called "Gun Smoke," dedicated to covering original and replica firearms and related gear for Old West enthusiasts, classic arms collectors, black powder buffs, and sport shooters. He writes for several other outdoor periodicals as well. Phil inspired the creation of an equestrian sport called "Cowboy Mounted Shooting." He is the Firearms Consultant for the Autry National Center. Spangenberger has been interviewed on the History Channel's *Tales of the Gun, Modern Marvels*, and *Wild West Tech* series. More recently, he has been serving as the Cavalry and Horse Coordinator for the *Conquerors* series, and has appeared in a number of episodes. Phil has served as a technical advisor, historical prop and gunleather supplier, and gun coach to such stars as Mel Gibson, Charlton Heston, Will Smith, Tom Beringer, and Ed Harris. He has worked on several box office hits such as *The Patriot*, where he taught Trevor Morgan and Heath Ledger, who played the hero's two young sons, how to fire a Brown Bess musket. The military standard during the time period being portrayed was to fire off three paper cartridge rounds per minute. "Even the little guy learned how to load and fire three rounds in one minute and ten seconds," Spangenberger grins. He has traveled to several different countries to do performances in Old West style, holding his reins in his teeth while performing trick shots at aerial targets. His wife, Linda, has won three Women's World Championship titles in the Cowboy Mounted Shooting Association (CMSA). She and fellow CMSA award-winning equestrienne Lori Brown perform riding sidesaddle at a full gallop, shooting balloon targets with their pistols. They are well-known participants at Equestfest.

Normally, *The Spirit of the West* group consists of 18 riders. Spangenberger places his most outgoing and personable riders toward the outside of the group, nearest the crowd. "On three, let's have a Happy New Year!" they call to the crowd. "One . . . two . . . three . . ." and the crowd shouts on cue. The riders encourage competition for volume between the two sides of the street. After so many years of this activity, today's crowds pick up the "one, two, three" chant before Phil's group even gets to their section.

Crowd members hold up signs to cheer the riders. "10½," they'll say, or "Only four more miles to go!" they'll joke, when the end of the Parade is near. The riders call back cheerfully, "We're ready!"

The Spirit of the West Riders have ridden in every parade since 1992.

One of Phil's favorite routines is to ride his big gray, Nevada, up close to the blue line that marks Parade riders' outer boundary and chat with people who have obviously spent the entire night on the Parade route and are still in their sleeping bags. He puts his hand on his holstered single-action Colt and grins, "Do you want me to put you out of your misery?" which always sparks a laugh. He never fires blanks in the Rose Parade, however, as that is against Tournament rules.

The first year the group participated, Phil recalls, "There was a big to-do about Columbus Day." A Native American rider in the group decided not to ride because Columbus's party had enslaved his people. Phil pointed out some of Columbus's achievements that were worth celebrating, as well as some of the less-than-humane activities that the Carib Indians practiced back then, but was unable to convince the fellow to stay. "No one is without sin," Phil comments. "And arguments should be based on reason, not hearsay." During that Parade, someone in the crowd held up a sign bearing a scatological description of Columbus. Protesters threw firecrackers under the horses' bellies in protest. Fortunately, Phil's horses were experienced with gunfire and didn't bolt. "Happy New Year," his riders yelled, as if the noise was in support of the Parade. Unfortunately, a woman mounted side-saddle on a mule in another equestrian group was bucked out of the saddle and

broke her arm because of the firecrackers. "Protesting is not what this Parade is about," Phil states emphatically. "People need to focus on why we're there. The whole day is about the fact that it's great to be alive!"

About seven or eight years ago, a float ahead of Spangenberger's group broke down and stopped the Parade just before Sierra Madre. A float with bungee-jumpers was positioned to the group's rear, and Phil turned his mount around in order to watch the jumpers. Suddenly his eyes met the eyes of a little ten year-old girl in the crowd. "Are you having a Happy New Year?" he asked her.

"It's my birthday today," she replied. "This is my birthday party."

Since the Parade had stopped and there was time to fill, Phil asked her if she'd like to have his group sing "Happy Birthday." The cowboy and cowgirl riders, on horseback, formed a semi-circle around her with their horses and sang to her while her dad videotaped their performance. Phil counts that moment as one of his favorite Parade memories, because he knows that the young lady has never forgotten that birthday.

One of Phil's more fearful Parade moments involved a rider by the name of Bill Kimmey, otherwise known as Standing Bear, Bill is in his 80s, now. He had had bypass surgery two months prior to the Parade, and had not informed Phil that he was a diabetic as well. Phil was concerned,

but Kimmey felt confident that he would be able to complete the Parade. About a fourth of the way into the route, however, Kimmey began to weave in his saddle. Phil told his Deputy Marshal, Larry Brady, to take charge of the group, and rode back to help Kimmey dismount. When his feet hit the street, Kimmey's legs buckled, and he sagged to the ground. The two horses stepped aside. People from the crowd came out to help pick up Kimmey's Indian gear for him. The paramedics arrived and took Kimmey away, and Phil took charge of the riderless mount, which had been rented for the Parade. His group was now about a block ahead of Phil's current position, so he took off at a lope to catch up with them. People in the crowd were cheering him on. As he continued along the route with the riderless horse, people shouted, "Hey! You're missing a rider."

"No, that's the Spirit of the West," he replied quickly.

When the group reached the end of the Parade, there sat Bill Kimmey, smiling. He had been given some juice to adjust his blood sugar level, and was just fine. "Here's your horse," Phil said as he handed over the reins.

Brian Flynn, development director at Huntington Medical Research Institute, is part of a three-generation connection with the Tournament of Roses and is a dedicated Tournament member. His mother rode in the parade back in the 1930s, and his godfather rode in the parade as well. Brian aspired to riding in the parade even as a child, and that vision has come to pass. Says he, "The Rose Parade is a way of bringing together people from all over and putting them up on these wonderful animals to share their beauty with the world." Brian's wife Robin is also a Tournament member. Brian rides with Spangenberger's *Spirit of the West* group when his Tournament duties will allow, dressing in authentic period costume along with the rest of the riders. He role-plays a vaquero from early California and does a one-man rodeo show, which is a bit of a history lesson about how the cowboy evolved in America out of Mexico. (Cowboys were

herding cattle in California before Washington crossed the Delaware.) In the 2004 parade he rode a huge thoroughbred Quarterhorse named Chief that measures 16 hands. The horse is primarily used as a rope horse, and can drag an uncooperative steer across an arena. They've done shows all over California, Arizona, and Colorado. Brian's voice goes soft with pride when he speaks of Chief: "He's big boy and pretty experienced. When we do a show, he'll snort and start to rear as part of the show, when in truth he's really extremely docile. When we start a parade, he plays a role too."

As with the rest of us who love the Tournament, New Year's

Eve for the equestrians is far too busy for parties and television. Brian describes it thus: "We come in to what we call 'The Pit' on New Year's Eve. It is a part of the 710, a four-lane highway that was never finished. Everyone comes in around 11:00 at night with tow vehicles and trailers, creating this enclave of equestrians. At about 6:30 or 7:00 you're brought up onto a little street called Waverly, where we form." (That operation, just as with all facets of the Parade, is all very organized, almost *ad nauseam*. The committee sends out notices to everyone asking what size trailer they're bringing and what they're towing it with. They chart the wide to narrow spaces

Equestrian Team of magnificent Andalusian Stallions from Medieval Times, 2004.

These colorfully painted horses represent those of a plains Indian tribe. Notice the center horse wears the fuzzy hair and horns of a buffalo!

(nearer to Colorado) of the area. They assign each tow vehicle and its trailer to a specific spot, based on size.)

"Until we get into the Parade itself," he continues, "we're separated from everything that's going on, and it feels like just another parade. But when the horse takes that first step onto Orange Grove Boulevard you're transformed. You feel as if you are the center of attention. The bands come up on Del Mar, and the horses come in on Waverly. It's hard to fathom the numbers of people, and so many VIPs recognize your group! There's a certain character to the parade on Orange Grove. VIP seating, television cameras, personalities — you're caught up in the spectacle. Everything needs to be just right, and you focus on detail.

"There's no preparing for the turn from Orange Grove to Colorado, though. The immensity of the audience! You're looking at five to ten times the number of people who will attend the Rose Bowl, and they're all waiting for you! The audience changes as you travel down Colorado — there are lots of children, many there for the first time. They're overawed by the huge floats, and the bands that span forever, and the tall, haughty horses. I've ridden close to the side, and my connection with the audience has been more intimate because of that. Lots of eye contact, a moment of recognition between two complete strangers. Eye contact with the kids produces a look of thankfulness that 'This cowboy recognizes me!' At that point there's at least five miles to go. You want to remember every step of the way, and all of a sudden you're at the freeway with only a few yards left before it's all over for that year."

He's right about the importance of eye contact with kids. I remember the 2005 trip to Osaka, Japan, where Megan Chinen (2004 Rose Queen) and I were privileged to ride in their parade. During the parade, Megan and I rode in a pristine Morgan convertible. The driver kept turning back and forth and driving to the edge of the crowd so that we could get closer to them. Megan had her crown on and was in her formal gown. She made eye contact with the kids in the crowd. She's of Pacific Rim Ancestry, and they responded to her with great interest and delight.

C. F. Brown, Marshal of the New Buffalo Soldiers, shares Brian's enthusiasm. He has been riding in the Rose Parade since 1995. The New Buffalo Soldiers are a non-profit mounted historical reenactment group with a mission to educate the public about Company H 10th Regiment of the U. S. Cavalry during the post-Civil War era and Indian Wars. Established in 1992, the riders represent a wide variety of occupations from medical professional to college student, but have a common passion for teaching history. They train their mounts and maintain their own historically correct equipment.

Brown, known to fellow equestrians as "Charlie," likes to feed his horses well before the parade. "A horse with a full stomach is more

This group riding Arabian horses is costumed in full Bedouin regalia.

relaxed," he instructs. Riders talk to horses to relax them, so Brown has his riders say the ABCs or count cadence. "I'm a horseshoer by trade," he says gently. The marshal of most equestrian groups rides at the front of the group, but Charlie prefers to blend in with his group because they represent a military presence, one of the all-black units that operated during the post-Civil War period. "The turn from Waverly onto the parade route is wonderful," he smiles. "And when you turn the corner onto Colorado, you are riding onto the floor of a huge canyon walled with people."

Slipping is a hazard for horses when they have to walk on asphalt, particularly if the street is wet or if one of the floats has leaked hydraulic fluid onto the pavement. A volunteer farrier comes to the "Pit" in the morning to check that the horses have been shod with borium to help stop the slipping. Brown explains it thus: "First you trim the foot. Then you shape the shoe to fit. Next you take a rod of borium and weld it onto the shoe using an acetylene torch. You put some across the toe, and a spot on either side of the heel. An alternative method, which I kind of prefer, is to drill four holes in the shoe — two in the toe and one on each side of the heel — and then tap in borium studs. This method assures that the horse's foot hits the ground level. The stuff really grips! In 1996 I did a horse with too much borium, and it fell. A third method is to use borium nails. The nails only last for one parade, though. The borium shoes can be used until you're ready to shoe the horse again, about six to eight weeks later."

Brown asserts that the way a horse is shod can help its gait. The secret lies in the angle of the foot and the size of the shoe. Good training is what perfects the gait. First, it's important to make a horse practice a good, long-reaching walk. That's the foundation. "A horse does what you train him to do," he insists. "Whether they know it or not, riders are cueing their horses the entire time they ride. Every rider is a trainer, good or bad!" Brown does a lot of leg work when he's riding — body contact is the communication channel.

Benny Martinez, Jr. has been riding in the Rose Parade for 25 years. He's the closest in experience to that of the late Monty Montana, whose last parade ride was in 1994, after 60 years of participation. (I still have one of Monty's signature small lassos in my office, as I was the Equestrian Chair that year.) Benny Martinez is a trick roper, often described as

Long Beach Mounted Police
This group of riders all decked out in red, white and blue carry American Flags and typify the traditional western equestrian parade unit. Their horses sport heavy, silver-bedecked tack.

"the finest trick roper alive," who twirls his rope constantly the entire length of the parade. His riders dress in authentic Mexican Charro suits dating back to the early 1800s, and ride atop hand-made Mexican saddles and side-saddles for the ladies. Benny is pretty serious about doing what he's expected to do during the parade. He waves at the crowd and says, "Happy New Year! God bless you!" They often ask him to stop and perform stunts, but he is very aware that the progress of the parade is timed to the second, and strives to be at the right place at the right time. Benny favors Azteca horses, which are half Andalusian and half Quarterhorse, but most of his shows have been with Napoleon, his trusty mustang. "Everything that we do is for the glory of our Father and our Savior Jesus Christ," he testifies. When asked how he manages to keep that rope spinning for two hours, he gives the credit to God.

The day before the parade we stage the Equestfest, which is a celebration of the equestrians in the parade. At one time we held it at Santa Anita Racetrack. Brian Flynn convinced me as to the validity of getting the horses out on the track. "I'm too big to ever be a jockey," he commented, and I could tell that he wanted to ride at the track. He had this vision that they'd give us the whole track, but they didn't. They barricaded it off at the stretch. The final year that we were there, however, we discovered as we came out on the track to rehearse that there were no barriers. Brian, who was

Benny Martinez spins a lariat throughout the entire parade, to the delight of the crowd.

riding his big paint quarter horse, sort of nudged his horse and went around the end. No one from the racetrack stopped them. Brian turned him around in the direction for racing and nudged him, and the horse was at a gallop in two strides, running 40 mph. People were cheering them on! His wife was up in the stands yelling, "That's my husband!"

The New Buffalo Soldiers, currently a group of 20 riders, usually act out a mock battle at the Equestfest. This is a true-to-life military maneuver where, when a rider comes under attack, he lays his horse down to be used as a barricade for protection against the hostiles. The remain-

ing troops ride out, pushing the hostiles back and rescuing the scout on the ground. This gives the scout the opportunity to re-mount. The troops then regroup and all ride away. Equestfest is also a place where participants can show off their roping skills and the special gaits and steps that their mounts have perfected.

Both Flynn and Brown love to play to the crowd. In 1997 the two teams playing at the Bowl were Arizona State and Ohio State. The colors were red and cardinal. We got into a delay, which occasionally happens. Brian found himself at a standstill right between grandstands full of people

Monty Montana, last of the "old time" Hollywood cowboy heros, was a regular feature of the parade.

Iron Eyes Cody, right, was also a frequent participant, a wonderful representative of the Native American Community who gained fame in the movies.

from the two schools on opposite sides of the street. Spontaneously, he turned to Ohio State's stand and shouted, "Who's going to win?" A roar of applause went up. Then he turned to Arizona to ask the same question, and they roared back. That started a contest that kept everyone's level of excitement up.

Something similar happened to me at the Kickoff Luncheon, which is a pep rally prior to the game. When I went to the stage to make my remarks, I asked how many fans were from Michigan. I got a pretty good response, so I asked how many were from USC. That got a better response. I went back and forth several times until we had the place in an uproar. But that was all right with everyone. After all, it was a pep rally!

Occasionally a spectator will try to cause trouble. White Suiters are constantly on the lookout for that. Brian Flynn recalls an incident that happened when he was in such a position. "I've only encountered trouble once. That year I was not riding, but doing a job as troubleshooter. I had a motorscooter and was watching for trouble. A couple of ill band members needed to get through the crowd to a van which shadows the parade. The crowd was thick. About eight guys were lining the sidewalk, and they wouldn't budge. They were, shall we say, 'chemically impaired.' Just then we had a delay in the parade for some reason. Four huge black horses happened to be right at that point, representing the Valley Hunt Club. The horse closest to the inebriated men stretched out and relieved himself. It was like a tsunami, and it headed right for them. They got up and scrambled away, leaving

The New Buffalo Soldiers reenact the roles of Company H 10th Regiment of the U. S. Cavalry during the post-Civil War era and Indian Wars.

The Valley Hunt Club uses beautiful, black Percherons to draw their antique carriage.

a space for the band members to get through. I thought to myself, 'There is a God, and He is just.'"

The crowds are not always noisy, by the way. Sometimes, during a lull, they can be downright quiet. Mel Smith describes one such moment: "One year I had duty on my Honda motorbike as a float escort. You have to realize that, in my white suit, I looked like the Michelin Tire snowman on a child's two-wheeled bicycle. My son, then about eight years old, was perched atop a lamppost at Oakland Avenue and Colorado Boulevard. The crowd had be-

come quite quiet. As I came riding around the end of the float, my son called out in a clear, high voice, "Do a wheely, Daddy!" The crowd, at least, found the concept quite funny."

If a horse gets sick during the parade, we're prepared with a whole slew of veterinarians and a horse ambulance which shadows the parade. Any horse requiring attention gets it quickly. We instruct equestrians to train their animals for the long ride without water, and to feed them and water them thoroughly before the parade begins. People who come to

the Tournament House often ask questions about the sanitation that goes with staging an event of this magnitude. They want to know how many PortaPotties we use, and what happens to the horse manure.

The *Wall Street Journal* published an article on December 30, 1969, entitled "Folks in Pasadena Say Running a Big Parade Is No Bed of Roses." The article's subtitle was "But They Tackle Menial Chores to Achieve Status in Town." Earl C. Gottschalk, Jr. reported that Peter Geddes, Jr., owner of Geddes Press in Pasa-

For some, pretty ladies and spirited horses are what the parade is all about.

This "Charro"- dressed woman shows off her horse's fancy footwork.

Eewwww!

The worst part of the parade was having to take extra-large steps to step over the horse dung.
—Carrie Richardson
Carrollton, Georgia

dena printing company, ". . . missed a Tournament of Roses committee meeting lately and got a big assignment for Thursday's Rose Parade." He continued, "Clad in the traditional white suit of Tournament staffers, he will perform before a national TV audience . . . His job: sweeping horse manure off the street to clean the area where pictures of the prize-winning floats are taken." Geddes and his wife had been vacationing in Hawaii after visiting their daughter in the Philippines, and missed the meeting where the "Pooper Scoopers" were assigned. There were 220 horses in the parade that year. The *Star-News* printed a picture of Geddes' face on its front page New Year's Day, captioned "What *is* he doing?" Readers who turned to page 13 of the paper found a four column-wide photograph of Geddes with his broom and scooper, with a pile of horse manure in the foreground. Geddes told the reporters, "No job is too menial if it helps the Tournament." And his wife told the *Star-News*, "The whole thing has provided amusement far out of proportion to its importance. But its very triviality has been a welcome relief from the usual stories of tragedy on the front pages. Thank you for entertaining so many." That's the kind of spirit Tournament members consistently display.

I once asked the vets how much solid waste a horse voids in a typical day, and how much that typically weighs. (C. F. Brown states it bluntly: "Horses are methane factories.") I then calculated the amount of manure produced in the 1994 parade. We had over 400 horses that year. I figured we could have spread the field of the Rose Bowl a foot and a half deep with the stuff. As Brian Flynn put it succinctly, "The horse poop elicits lots of response from the crowd. They watch to see if the kids walk in a straight line or step around."

Down at the other end of the parade route, when it's all over, equestrians and band members get treated to an In-N-Out Burger. The company sets up a 40-foot trailer with nine separate grills, each of which can produce 250 cheeseburgers per hour. They fix about 10,000 burgers, all told. Managers from local stores vie to come in and cook on that day, and they are careful that every burger reaches its recipient steaming hot. (Burgers that cool because of a lag in the marchers' lines are discarded.) Each band member and equestrian gets a burger, a bottle of water, and an apple. Three of the bands, the Marine Corps band and the two university bands, get two hamburgers per member because they have to hurry on to the police-escorted convoy to be transported for their performance at the Rose Bowl. It is not uncommon to observe a petite female band member who has refused a second burger being approached by a hungry male who advises, "Go ahead and take the second one! I'll be glad to take care of it for you!"

The horses are usually pretty happy to head for their trailers. The parade ends, as it began, in a residential area. People give up space in front of their homes so the horses' chauffeurs can park their rigs.

It's a great treat to see how the community offers up their streets for them. I've never heard a resident complain. They buy into it, and it was part of the tradition when they bought their homes. It's a time for them to be part of what we do in Pasadena. Everybody on Orange Grove has a party New Year's Eve. Mel Smith tells a story about how he and Jim McAdam were manning the phones at the Tournament House one year. Jim received a call from a distressed lady who owned a home on Del Mar near Orange Grove. She reported that a young couple had spread blankets out on her new front lawn and were doing unspeakable things. She wanted us to do something about it.

Jim responded, "Ma'am, have you tried calling the police?"

"Yes, but they haven't done anything about it. Can you please help remove them from my lawn?"

"No, Ma'am," said Jim, "but why don't you try turning on your lawn sprinklers?"

This rider playfully "ropes" a photographer along the parade route.

These Tournament volunteer "pooper-scoopers" wear much deserved "halos."

CHAPTER 8
Of Queens and Crowns

Mike Riffey and his Royal Court in 2004.

Of Queens and Crowns

Rich Chinen's professional specialty is family law and estate planning in Pasadena. His wife Kim works at Pasadena Christian School in the Admissions Department. Rich has been a Member-at-Large on the Executive Committee and now serves as a Committiee Chair, which takes both talent and business acumen. His daughter Megan was the Queen of the Tournament of Roses in 2004. It was an unusual situation for the Chinen family, as Megan's identical twin sister Erin had also tried out for Queen.

A nine-member committee selects the Rose Queen and her Royal Court. Gene Gregg was the chair of the Queen and Court Committee for the 2004 Tournament. The 2004 Rose Princesses were Christina Mills, a senior at La Salle High School in Pasadena; Natalie Matsumoto, a senior at San Marino High School; Erinne La Brie, a senior at Arcadia High School; Laura Stassel, a senior at Flintridge Sacred Heart Academy; Katie Koch, a senior at John Marshall Fundamental High School in Pasadena; and Stephanie Barnes, a senior at La Canada High School. Megan Chinen, a senior at La Salle High School, was chosen as Rose Queen. She is gracious, articulate, and poised, just like all the other girls. Any one of them could have done it, but Megan has a special flair. I saw it both during the Parade and afterward, when we traveled to Japan. Anywhere she was, she could take care of herself with eloquence. I hope that she'll take this throughout her life.

To the Manor Born

Every year since 1929, Rose Queens and Rose Princesses have been part of the Tournament of Roses. The seven members of the Royal Court attend a variety of social and media functions as ambassadors of the Tournament and the city of Pasadena. They become overnight celebrities. Media interviews, photo sessions, appearances with the Rose Parade Grand Marshal, visits to area service clubs, greeting the Rose Bowl football teams, and meetings with Rose Parade participants keep them busy in the months following Royal Court announcement day.

The grand finale of their reign, of course, is the ride down Colorado Boulevard in the Rose Parade as the multitudes of curbside spectators and television audiences across the world look on. Later, the Royal Court reigns over the Rose Bowl Game, seen by more than 93,000 in-person spectators and millions of television viewers.

Following each round of interviews, participants are notified by mail if they are being invited to the next interview session. Participants are evaluated on a wide range of qualities, including academic achievement, poise, personality, public speaking ability, and appearance. As part of the process, they meet previous Royal Court members, make new friends, and learn about Pasadena's tradition of the Tournament of Roses.

Once members of the Royal Court are selected, their schools' officials are contacted and informed about the various activities in which the girls will be involved. In the weeks following the Royal Court selection, time may be required during school hours for wardrobe fittings, photography sessions, and media appearances. Many of the Royal Court functions are purposely scheduled during the winter vacation period.

The girls were provided with a new wardrobe by Macy's of Pasadena, and had their hair and nails styled by Amadeus Spa of Pasadena. They were coached in speech, protocol, and media relations.

I can't imagine the tension and excitement of having not one, but two daughters in the competition. My own daughter tried out for the Court, and I am glad that I wasn't on the committee then. When she rode with me in the 2004 President's car years later, she said to me, "Dad, I knew this was big, but I didn't understand how big!"

I asked Rich Chinen to contribute some comments for this book so that you could see from his perspective not only what we do, but why we do it. When I described the plan for *More Than a Parade*, he responded, "The title just fits! So many times when you take on a task, it's a lot of work. I became a member in 1989. People asked me where I'd like to go when I got off the Executive Committee. I'd like to get back into the Parade. I first served on the Music Committee, and people kept telling me what a wonderful committee it was. I was dying because it was so much work! But afterward, when I saw it come together so beautifully, with all the potential nightmares that didn't happen, I was so proud and impressed. It gets in your blood.

"One time Mike was here to meet eleven band directors who had come out in 2003 to see where they would be marching in 2004. It was my job to put that reception together. We were going to have a bus tour of the Parade route. We were so pumped up! Mike got the guys going. Andy Soucy got up and said, "The kids you bring to this parade will never look at New Year's Day the same way again in their entire lifetime."

Rich's wife Kim describes the Queen competition in a soft voice: "The group of gals that tried out was over 1,000. For all intents and purposes, the twins look exactly alike. They're very different inside, but they look alike. Their little circle of friends came to the try-outs together, except that Erin had a commitment that day and came separately. Megan went through on one day, Erin on the next. Both came home after their respective interview and said, 'There's no way! These girls are fabulous!' It's not a beauty contest or a brains contest, but how you speak on your feet to the world. It's a 20-second spot. You walk through and say your number and one other thing. It's not the stereotypical beauty pageant. One girl said, 'I'm surprised I'm here, because I'm a jock.' Yes, the girls are beautiful, but the judges look for the way they communicate and radiate the joy of being part of something that's so much bigger than they are. These judges have a daunting task. The girls are fabulous and beautiful. They're the top of their schools, but the judges don't know all of that."

I served on the selection committee in 1982 and 1983, and Kim is right: the judges don't know all about each girl who tries out. In fact, if you do know or recognize a candidate, you disqualify yourself and that young lady gets the average of the other judges' score added on.

"It truly is fair," continues Kim. "Both of our girls made it through two levels of tryouts. Only Megan made it to the third level, and that was a correct choice. Megan has special gifts that applied to this situation. Erin has other gifts. She is very involved in sports, Advanced Placement, and honors classes. She could only try out as number 800 or something in the line of candidates, because she was at a volleyball tournament the first part of the tryouts. She is an excellent athlete, and would have missed out on CIF finals in badminton and soccer if she had been on the Court. Megan was a cheerleader, and missed out on some of those activities when she was being interviewed."

"It's really a rite of passage," Rich notes. "If you try out, you get to go to the Royal Ball. Some people try out just to get tickets."

"That's what I did 35 years ago! That's all I cared about," laughs Kim.

There were 41 days of school left after the names of the girls selected for the Court were announced, and Megan missed some school time at 39 of those. She had to exercise a great deal of self-discipline to keep up with her college prep and Advanced Placement classes. Rich and Kim felt that it was their role as parents to support her and make sure that she stayed healthy. Pasadena is a small enough community that only 26 public and private high schools and the city college are represented. The schools are excited when one of their students makes it. Both the principal and the president of Megan's school called the Chinens to congratulate them and share their excitement. The entire student body and faculty pledged to offer whatever help they could. It was helpful that the twin sisters were in the same classes; Erin's notes helped Megan immensely when she had to miss classes.

When Megan got to the finals, 30 girls were out standing on the south steps of the Tournament House. Kim looked at all of them and thought to herself, "This is not real." She had grown up in the Pasadena area, and she was married to someone who had volunteered for many years. "It seemed impossible that it was happening to *us*!"

After the officials announced the names of all the finalists, the parents were ushered in to a meeting. It was explained that, for several weeks at least, the Tournament would see more of the Royal Court than their families would. The complexity of the information and the intensity of the Court's schedule was a bit daunting, and Kim had a flash of motherly concern. "I don't know these nine people who are going to be in charge of her if she is selected, but I can trust them because I believe in the Tournament of Roses family." They did, in effect, become Megan's surrogate parents for that interim. Kim settled her own mind: "I know what they represent and what they stand for. She's going to grow and have experiences that we could never have dreamed of."

ELIGIBILITY REQUIREMENTS

To be eligible for the Royal Court, participants must meet all of the following requirements:

The Tournament of Roses Royal Court selection process is open to all unmarried women who have not previously been married, have no children, and who agree not to marry before January 2, 2005.

Participants must be legal residents of the Trustee Areas of the Pasadena Area Community College District.

Each participant must be enrolled as a senior in high school or as a full-time college student (minimum 12 units) in an accredited school or college within the Trustee Areas of the Pasadena Area Community College District.

Participants must demonstrate that they have earned at least a 2.0 ("C") grade point average (GPA) in the current and previous year's course work.

Participants must be at least 17 years of age by December 31 of the preceding year and not more than 21 years of age before January 2 of the parade year.

Each participant must complete an official application and participate in one of the initial interview sessions.

There is one week between the announcement of the Court and the selection of the Queen. All of the girls on the Court are taken to a house in Balboa and taught how to walk, how to make conversation, and how to get in and out of a van like a lady. Upon their return, they are introduced to the entire Executive Committee. Each girl is brought down the Tournament House steps on the arm of a Tournament member. That ceremony was very special for me, because it was "my" Court. The girls were so lovely! They had been transformed completely, like ducklings into swans.

Rich describes it this way: "It was almost unbelievable how beautiful they looked and how poised they were. The judges were looking for young women who are articulate, bright, and charming. If someone sticks a microphone in front of one of their faces, the young lady has to be able to say something meaningful. I didn't know whom they had chosen, but I was aware that my life and my daughter's life might change dramatically in the course of a few minutes. It's a mixed feeling."

The first person announced was from La Salle High School, where Megan and Erin attend, and it wasn't Megan, so Rich and Kim figured right away that Megan wouldn't be chosen. The second person chosen was of Pacific Rim Ancestry, as are the Chinens, so they figured that for sure there would be no chance. And then, to their amazement

and thrill, Megan was the third person announced! It was a telling moment for the twin sisters. A photographer from the *LA Times* caught a shot of Erin and Megan with their heads together, puffy-eyed from tears. Erin comments on the emotion: "I knew that I wasn't going to have my sister around much for the next few months." Erin had been selected by the high school yearbook staff as "best personality." Megan was voted as "most spirited," — she's

A stranger came up to me once because she saw my President's pin. She wanted me to know how valuable the training is for the girls in the Royal Court. "My daughter is now a vice president at Mattel," she said. "She can get up and speak in front of thousands of people without batting an eye. Thank you for that."
—Mike Riffey

a bit more reserved, but the two girls are inseparable. They realized that they would be missing each other quite a lot.

The Court is selected on a Monday. By Thursday night, they have been prepared to get up in front of 75 people and give speeches! They're kids, ages 17, 18, 19 — and in a very short period of time they become adults. It is compelling to sit and listen to their articulate comments, anywhere from two to five min-

utes in length. Here were seven young ladies who were going to represent the Tournament for a lifetime. They just took off. The seven of them were absolutely themselves — none of them had notes. Kim recalls the intensity of her emotions: "I couldn't even put on a darn necklace, because I was so nervous and teary. I couldn't believe that my daughter was having this experience. It is so healthy, and so transforming."

Rich adds, "We were sitting at the table with Dave and Holly Davis, 2005 President. Dave saw that Megan had made some notes. He grabbed them from her as a joke. She gave her speech without them, even though Dave offered them back at the last minute."

For the announcement of the Queen's selection, the Chinens found themselves back on the Tournament House lawn at 9:30 in the morning, and it was a hot day. The girls were in blazers, and they were just dying from the heat. Now the media were in the middle of things. There were so many that they were on risers. Rick was wandering on the grounds. Erin has an interest in broadcast journalism, and was covering the event for Lancer TV, the high school's television station. Adria deBaca invited Erin into the media box with the rest of the journalists. The media are informed of the judges' selection five seconds before the Queen is announced, so that they can zoom in on the correct face. Erin was handed an announcement sheet with the pictures of the

At the moment of the announcement of the 2004 Rose Queen's name. Megan Chinen and her court react.

Erin and her twin sister, Rose Queen Megan, share a hug at a press event.

©L.A. Times

A Rose by 7 Other Names

Erin Chinen, right, hugs her twin sister, Megan, who was among seven young women named to the 2004 Tournament of Roses Royal Court. Megan, 17, is a senior at La Salle High. Also among 37 finalists were Stephanie Barnes, 17, La Cañada High; Katherin... Fundamental High; Erinne La Brie, 17, Arcadia High; Natalie Matsumoto... Christina Mills, 17, La Salle High; and Laura Stassel, 17, Flintridge Sacred...

ANNIE WELLS Los Angeles Times

The Royals goof around in their rose-covered PJs.

Photo by Kathy Matsumoto

Just minutes into her reign, Queen Megan faces questions from the press.

During my first year of attendance at Pasadena City College, the Tournament of Roses tryouts occurred during P. E. classes. It happened that I made the first elimination before the judges; however, I didn't return for the next tryout. The following year, in October of 1954, I decided to go on with the event. It seemed to me the chances of becoming the 1955 Rose Queen were quite slim, as there were 1,800 women students in the first elimination.

It is hard to imagine how proud and honored I felt that day when I was named the Tournament of Roses Queen! My dear family and friends shared in the excitement of this noble honor. Over the years I have striven to uphold the outstanding standards of the Tournament. And I have become like an ambassador as I give gifts of felt lapel roses or pins to others, sharing this honor with them.

Close ties of friendship have occurred with the former queens and the Tournament, and with Eastman Kodak.

The most outstanding moment of my reign was on January 1, 1955, as the Rose Queen float made it through a misty morning. It happened to rain on my parade, although they called it a "fine mist." Nevertheless, the cheering crowd, on a darkened day, brought sunshine to my soul and warmed my heart.

—Marilyn Soniun Beutler
Rose Queen, 1955

girls marked with a circle or an x, and thus found out that her sister would be the Queen before anyone else in the family knew. "That shows how the people who work here are in tune with our whole family," Kim muses. "Then they announced Megan, and I was having that out-of-body feeling again, wondering where my husband was. Then they ushered the girls inside, and no media were admitted at first except for Erin. I am so proud to be part of an organization that considers the family more important than the job to be done."

When the girls are selected to the Royal Court, the parents find out that the girls have over 100 appearances to attend. Both Erin and Megan were on the homecoming court for their school, and it conflicted with one of the appearances. Now the Tournament is important, but the girls are still high school students. Megan was senior class president, and felt that she would be letting the student body down if she did not attend Homecoming. She said, "I really don't care about being the Queen. I am just so tickled to be on the Court!" The chairman called Rich and said, "She can miss Saturday night if you'll do the driving." Rich knew that she'd be missing out on the skit that the girls do in front of the selection committee, and that this would probably cost her any chance to be Queen. But she wanted to go, so he did the six hours of driving. After all of that, Megan was very shocked when her name was announced as Queen. When she and the other girls huddled together after the announcement, she said, "Remember what we said before one of us was chosen — Nothing changes!" And so they all shouted together "Nothing changes."

Megan was taken upstairs immediately to do a commercial or something. One of the other six said, "I'm hungry." So someone went back to get a couple of baskets of munchies. One of the girls sitting around the table said, "You know, Megan's the right girl." I was amazed! They all agreed that the committee had made the right choice. The committee stresses this with them: the Queen has a different title, but is just one of the entire Court. No one is more important than the other.

Megan's duties as a celebrity began right away. Rick recalls his apprehension: "Megan and I were waiting outside before an entrance to a tent on the Tournament House lawn. A reporter and a cameraman came running across the lawn. The girls had been isolated at Balboa, and I knew that they hadn't listened to much news. The reporter said, 'Queen Megan, what would you like to say to all the fire victims out there?' I panicked, because I doubted that Megan had even heard that there were fires going on in California. Without skipping a beat, she said, 'I just hope that you all know that we are all praying for you.' Right after the coronation, she and Mike went down to the Rose Bowl and she presented a $5,000 donation from the Tournament to the fire victims, where donors were gathering. She had her crown and her gown on, and she knelt down to talk with every one of those little kids."

The 2004 Queen and Princesses have remained close ever since the Parade. When we went to Osaka, Japan in October, 2005, a young lady from the Aquatennial/ Minnesota was there. They all went earlier, and Megan and I went together about an hour later. The young lady from the Aquatennial got out of the car. Megan didn't choose to get out yet. The young lady was immediately swarmed around her to get a picture, and we saw her face go white with panic. Megan said, "She needs help!" These are young women, and we always need to make sure that they are safe and no one injures or harms them in any way. We stepped out, and Megan helped her handle the crowd.

Kim Chinen recalls that the late Holly Balthis would come to the coronation luncheon whenever possible. She was beautifully coifed and perfectly dressed each time. "I watched Holly over the past 15 years," Kim insists. "There was something different about her. I wished I could meet her now and talk to her. I wanted to tell her how I've watched her all these years, how regal her presence is." Kim eventually did get the chance to visit with Holly. "I told her how I revered her attitude and behavior, and how glad I was that our daughter was a part of this whole tradition now. She let me get a picture of Megan and her.

"We went down to her funeral service, and the thread throughout the service was her regal presence. There was a basket of single red roses at the entrance to the church. Everybody that was a princess or queen was asked to take a rose. When we left, there were only two roses remaining in the basket. People came from all over the country to celebrate Holly's life. She was the benchmark for all who came after her. As time passes, the memory becomes sweeter and sweeter. You say, "Wow! I was a part of this!"

When The Heritage Committee was putting together the museum they asked the past Queens to donate their gowns for a display at the museum. They didn't hear from Holly and someone called. She kind of hesitated, and then shared the story that she made her dress and decorated her own car for the parade back then. Later, when she was looking for a job and going on interviews, she had to use the valuable Rose Queen gown material to make a blouse to go with her first suit.

ONCE MORE INTO THE BRA-EACH

It was exactly 4:30 a.m. the morning of the 1980 Tournament of Roses Parade. The Queen and her Royal Entourage were gathered in the Queen's Room. It was a joyous occasion. Hairstylists were busy with curlers and combs. Makeup artists were applying lipstick and rouge. Couteriers were active with needles and thread and steam irons, making final form-fitting adjustments. Suddenly there was a gasp and a stifled scream from Princess Mary McCoy. She called out to me, "Mr. Hemmings, I forgot my bra!" It was too late to go home and retrieve the accessory. What to do?

Peggy Hemmings stepped into the breach, asking Mary, "What is your size?"

With the question answered, Peggy led Mary to a private room. Minutes later they emerged, Mary wearing Peggy's brassiere and Peggy sans said accessory. The two were a perfect match!

An emergency such as this is why wives of Queen and Court Committee members are included in all functions dealing with the ladies of the court.

—Bob Hemmings

PASADENA TOURNAMENT OF ROSES QUEENS
THROUGH THE YEARS

1890 - 1904 No Queens
1905 Hallie Woods
1906 Elsie Armitage
1907 Joan Woodbury
1908 May Sutton
1909 - 1910 No Queens
1911 Ruth Palmer
1912 No Queen
1913 Jean P. French
1914 Mabel Seibert
1915 - 1922 No Queens
1923 May McAvoy
1924 No Queen
1925 Margaret Scoville
1926 Fay Lanphier
1927 No Queen
1928 Harriet Sterling
1929 No Queen
1930 Holly Halsted
1931 Mary Lou Waddell
1932 Myrta Olmsted
1933 Dorothy Edwards
1934 Treva Scott
1935 Muriel Cowan
1936 Barbara Nichols
1937 Nancy Bumpus
1938 Cheryl Walker
1939 Barbara Dougall
1940 Margaret Huntley
1941 Sally Stanton
1942 Dolores Brubach
1943 Mildred Miller
1944 Naomi Riordan
1945 Mary Rutte
1946 Patricia Auman
1947 Norma Christopher
1948 Virginia Goodhue
1949 Virginia Bower
1950 Marion Brown
1951 Eleanor Payne
1952 Nancy Thorne
1953 Leah Feland
1954 Barbara Schmidt
1955 Marilyn Smuin
1956 Joan Culver
1957 Ann Mossberg
1958 Gertrude Wood
1959 Pamela Prather

MRS. ELMER WOODBURY
1907

HOLLY HALSTED
1930

MARGARET HUNTLEY
1940

SALLY STANTON
1941

DOLORES J. BRUBACH
1942

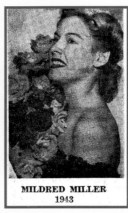
MILDRED MILLER
1943

NORMA CHRISTOPHER
1947

VIRGINIA GOODHUE
1948

Photos of some of the Rose Queens as they appeared in the newspaper.

Tournament President C. Elmer Anderson and three Rose Queens.

The Queen, Fay Lanphier and her court in 1926.

1935 Queen, Muriel Cowan and Tournament officials pose at the Tournament House.

1969 Grand Marshall, Bob Hope charms a bevy of Royal Court candidates.

The 2004 Royal Court pauses on the Tournament House steps for a photo before proceeding to their float on parade day.

All the living Rose Queens pose together on the day of the Queens' Luncheon. 2004 Queen Megan Chinen (top row center) is the newest, youngest queen on this day. Holly Halsted-Balthis is the oldest, pictured in the front row farthest right.

1960 Margarethe Bertelson
1961 Carole Washburn
1962 Martha Sissell
1963 Nancy Davis
1964 Nancy Kneeland
1965 Dawn Baker
1966 Carole Cota
1967 Barbara Hewitt
1968 Linda Strother
1969 Pamela Anicich
1970 Pamela Tedesco
1971 Kathleen Arnett
1972 Margolyn Johnson
1973 Salli Noren
1974 Miranda Barone
1975 Robin Carr
1976 Anne Martin
1977 Diane Ramaker
1978 Maria Caron
1979 Catherine Gilmour
1980 Julie Raatz
1981 Leslie Kawai
1982 Katherine Potthast
1983 Suzanne Gillaspie
1984 Ann Marie Colborn
1985 Kristina Smith
1986 Aimee Richelieu
1987 Kristin Harris
1988 Julie Myers
1989 Charmaine Shryock
1990 Yasmine Delawari
1991 Cara Rullman
1992 Tannis Turrentine
1993 Liana Yamasaki
1994 Erica Brynes
1995 Aliya Haque
1996 Keli Hutchins
1997 Jennifer Halferty
1998 Purdy Tran
1999 Christina Farrell
2000 Sophia Bush
2001 Michelle Jacobs
2002 Caroline Hsu
2003 Alexandra Wucetich
2004 Megan Chinen
2005 Ashley Moreno
2006 Camille Clark

The Rose Queen, Margaret Scoville and her Royal
Court ride down Colorado Boulevard in 1925.

September 3, 1992

Dear Caryn:

I hasten to comply with your request, and as you probably know, my year 1930, began the unbroken line of succession of Rose Queens.

My association with the Tournament of Roses, having personally known every Queen since Hallie Woods McConnell, a brother in law, Paul S. Bryan (President 1975), riding in numerous parades, has made an enduring and lasting impression on my life.

While I was not born in Hallie's reign, I met and became friends in later years with every Rose Queen including Joan Woodbury, May Sutton Bundy, Harriet Sterling (my Junior High School teacher) and Dr. F. C. E. Mattison, the only King of the T.R., who delivered me into this world in Pasadena in 1908 in a cottage on Granite Drive, where the Chronicle Restaurant now stands.

One of the rewards of being the Oldest Living Rose Queen is to meet each incoming Queen and to welcome her into our exclusive organization of former Rose Queens. She learns that she is not only a queen for a day, but for a lifetime.

I am still taking an active part in attending coronations, Junior Chamber breakfasts, Kodak luncheons, speaking engagements before various service clubs, City and Tournament Centennials, the Good Sam R. V.'ers, the Crown City Chorus and lately, the Kodak and Rose Milk floats in the Parade.

I wish to thank the Tournament for its cooperation in the use of the Wrigley Mansion for our reunions, and in particular, Frosty, in making us feel so at home. I was in charge of the June 20th Rose Queen reunion at Tournament House. I sent fifty-five invitations to former queens and received, in return, forty replies or regrets, evidence that the past queens have kept their interest in representing the T. of R. We are a loving group of friends who owe much to the Queens selection Committee who have used good judgement through the years.

If, in any way, I can be of assistance you only have to call on

—Holly Halsted Balthis
(Mrs. Frank Balthis)

Holly Halsted-Balthis and her husband, Frank Balthis ride in the parade in 1975.

Former Rose Queens, (standing, left to right) Norma Christopher Winton, 1947; Joan Culver Warren, 1956; Nancy Davis Maggio, 1963; and (seated) Holly Halsted Balthis, 1930, examine the Queen's gown for 1963.

Holly Balthis remained a beauty, and throughout her life continued to actively participate in the Tournament and Rose Queen activities.

©Pasadena Star News

Rose Queens Megan Chinen, 2004, and Holly Halsted Balthis, 1930, pose together.

HOLLY HALSTED BALTHIS, above, was crowned Rose Queen in 1930. At top, she is seen with 2004 Rose Queen Megan Chinen. Balthis was involved with the Tournament of Roses and mentored new Rose Queens her entire adult life.

This picture of Holly Halsted Balthis, during her reign in 1930 appeared in the **Pasadena Star News** to memorialize her at her passing in 2004.

Tadashi calls his entrance into the world of design a "true accident." Born in Japan, he became an artist at an early age, and enjoyed all aspects of art. He applied to an art school, but was not one of the five out of every five hundred applicants chosen. He then worked with avant garde conceptual artist Jiro Takamatsu, who is still working in Japan, but couldn't make a career out of that type of art. His sister is a fashion designer in Japan, and perhaps that swayed his interests.

At twenty-five years of age, a Japanese male without a career is somewhat an outcast, so Tadashi left Japan and "ran away" to Los Angeles. He couldn't afford to enroll in an expensive art school, so he began studying at Los Angeles Trade Technical College. When he enrolled, he said, "I didn't know the meaning of a dart," but he was intrigued with shaping vibrant colored fabrics to women's bodies and the draping of fabrics became another kind of art for the talented student.

After a variety of jobs, he was hired by Mr. Blackwell of the "Worst-Dressed" lists who had a small, high-end company. During the second semester at L.A. Trade Tech, he applied for a job with Bill Whitton, a costume designer for television specials featuring the likes of Stevie Wonder, Neil Diamond, the Jackson Five and The Commodores. He worked four years as an assistant to Mr. Whitton, designing costumes for chorus girls and showbiz notables while he attended school in the mornings. When he tried to join the garment trade which specialized in mass production in downtown Los Angeles, he was told that because of his couture-type designing, he needed to apply elsewhere.

After this period, Tadashi joined a business partner, who, when they had met, sold fabrics. Together, they

OFFICIAL DESIGNER FOR THE ROSE PARADE QUEEN AND HER COURT

designed, sewed, and marketed their clothing line for seventeen years. Today, Tadashi is designer/president of his own design corporation, simply known as Tadashi.

His philosophy of design is simply that the women who wear his dresses on a special day or night must be comfortable physically and mentally.

He started designing gowns for the Rose Parade Queens and Court fourteen years ago. The first four years he competed with two other designers, and was chosen to design for the Queen and the Royal Court each year. By the fifth year, he had become the official designer for the Rose Parade.

Designing the dresses for the Rose Queen and her Court begins in June or July when the President's for the coming year and spouse, visit the company in Vernon, California where Tadashi works his magic. Tadashi presents several original drawings for the president's wife to look at and decide which design will grace the Queen and Court. They then choose the color for the Court, which is different every year. The Queen's dress is always white, usually silk, and the Courts' gowns are taffeta or polyester, fabrics which lend themselves to bright colors.

Tadashi's gowns can be found in most upscale retailers worldwide such as Neiman Marcus, Sak's, Bloomingdale's, Macy's, Nordstrom's, and some specialty boutiques including The Forum at Caesar's in Las Vegas and South Coast Plaza. Many Hollywood stars, international performers, and politicians, some of which are Halle Berry, Celine Dion, Catherine Zeta-Jones, and Condolezza Rice have worn his creations, and he has costumed five lovely presenters of Oscars. He is the designer for the movie remake of *Poseidon*.

MIKIMOTO AMERICA, DESIGNER AND MAKER OF THE 2005 ROSE QUEEN CROWN

Robert Artelt, Senior Vice President of Marketing and Retail for Mikimoto (America) Co., Ltd., the Originator of Cultured Pearls since 1893, had a personal excitement about the lovely crown given to the Tournament of Roses 2005 Rose Queen. He recalled marching in the Rose Parade in 1975 as a trumpeter in the John Hersey High School band from Arlington Heights, Illinois. As the thirtieth anniversary of his experience neared, he thought of the natural connection between Mikimoto and the Rose Parade: A pearl is the jewel which commemorates a thirtieth anniversary, and is a natural object, much like the flowers used to decorate the Rose Parade floats.

When asked about how Mikimoto became involved with making the 2005 Tournament of Roses crown, Artelt said there were a number of factors. Mikimoto has a long history of crafting tierras and crowns for the Imperial Family in Japan. Tadashi, the official designer of the gowns for the Rose Queen and her Royal Court, as well as for the Miss U.S.A. Pageant, and familiar with their work, suggested to Mikimoto Co., Ltd., that they make a new crown for the Rose Queen as they had for Miss U.S.A. In addition, Mikimoto has a history of creating commemorative event crowns. In 1957, the company donated cherry trees to the Capital, and the crown to the Washington D.C. Cherry Blossom Festival Queen. A Mikimoto crown for the Tournament of Roses Queen and tierras for her Princesses seemed an excellent idea.

Amy Kim-Araneo, Design and Product Development Director for Mikimoto, worked with the Design Team in Japan and used the elegant overlapping heart motif to signify love and to highlight a halo effect. It was hand-made by Mikimoto's Master Jeweler in their factory in Japan. When not being worn, will be on display in one of four Mikimoto U.S. Retail Stores: Fifth Avenue, New York; The Regent Beverly Wilshire, Beverly Hills; South Coast Plaza, Costa Mesa and the Venetian Resort Hotel and Casino, Las Vegas.

The Queen and her Royal Court are temporary "owners" of these crowns, but this year they got a lasting gift. Each girl was given a Mikimoto pearl necklace which was presented by each girl's mother at the President's Luncheon. The father or other close male family member usually walks each girl in, and the mothers have been in the audience. The change this year created a great deal of emotion and created a bond between the mothers and daughters, and will become a tradition, both for Mikimoto and the families involved with the Tournament of Roses. Additionally, the mothers were given pearl brooches in 2006.

This beautiful diamond crown is last used in 2004 for the coronation of Queen Megan Chinen. Megan is crowned by Mike Riffey on coronation day.

Other crowns on this page were used in (from top) 1993–2004, 1968, 1954-1967, 1936–1938 and 1940–1943.

CHAPTER 9

Every Float
Is a Winner

Gateway to California Dreamin'

ONT 4 FUN

ont

GOVERNOR'S TROPHY
LIFE IN CALIFORNIA

Raul Rodriguez, with his macaw Sebastion, rides on his City of Whittier float he designed for 2005.

Every Float Is a Winner

Every seven years, Raul R. Rodriguez shares his January 2nd birthdate with the Rose Parade. Coincidence, perhaps? Or destiny? Rodriguez believes in both fate and destiny, and a good deal of self-motivation.

When a kindergarten teacher noticed that Raul, at age four and a half, was drawing in a manner that was advanced for that age, she informed Raul's parents that their child was a gifted artist. Perhaps the talent sprang from his great-uncle, Galileo Cortez, who painted for California's land grant families. Raul's parents made sure that he had ample supplies of pencils and sketch paper, as well as books about art and artists. His parents moved from East Los Angeles to Norwalk when he was in his early teens. "They bought a house that, had it been one block further up the street, would have put me in a different high school district. I attended Santa Fe High, part of the Whittier Union High School District." The Whittier Chamber of Commerce held a float design contest each year among area high schools; at the age of 14 Raul submitted an entry. He won the competition that year, and the year after. That was the beginning.

"The Rose Parade is about bringing the world together," he explains. "I began to understand it many years ago when I heard that a friend's mother on the East Coast was so touched by FTD's *Happy Birthday, America* float that she photographed it off her television set and hung the picture on her wall. It made a difference to her. As long as I'm alive, I hope to make a difference." A third-generation Angelino, Raul did not grow up speaking Spanish, but he has learned to speak the language fluently in order to represent his heritage more fully. He has served in the past as a guest anchor on Univision, and that year they won an Emmy for their Parade coverage.

Raul recalls a moment when he was riding a parade float that approached the turn from Colorado Boulevard onto Sierra Madre with too much speed. Almost losing his balance, he had to stretch quickly to keep from losing his blue hyacinth macaw, Roxie. "Suddenly I found myself looking directly into the faces of a group of wheelchair-bound observers who had been seated at the edge of the parade route. Up to that point, I had been concerned with the fact that we had not taken the top prize. When I saw their faces just looking for a smile, I re-evaluated what is really important. For me, the floats represent an opportunity to make the world more beautiful, and to capture life's moments of beauty."

A classically trained artist in drawing and painting, Rodriguez graduated from Cerritos College and California State University at Long Beach. A scholarship to the Art Center in Los Angeles allowed him to take additional life study classes. "If you can portray the human body from any perspective, using any light source, there is not a thing on the planet you won't be able to capture," he instructs. He traveled by bus to classes, and passed Windsor Square in Hancock Park along the way. "That's where I want to live some day," he told his parents, and they encouraged him to follow his dreams.

Soon he was working as a designer for Walt Disney Imagineering. Next he was hired by Heath and Company to produce electrical signage. At age 19, he submitted a design for the porte cochere and sign

Below, sketches of proposed floats by Raul Rodrguez.

Love Songs

SWEEPSTAKES TROPHY
MOST BEAUTIFUL

Floats run the gamut from the sublime to the
ridiculous, as evidenced by the Sweepstakes
Trophy winner above and the entry sporting
this explosive plumbing incident.

façade of the Las Vegas Flamingo Hilton for Baron Hilton. That design has now become an icon that is visible for miles across the desert. "Here I was, too young to drink or gamble, which I still don't do, with a down payment check for $150,000.00 for the first million-dollar sign spectacular in Las Vegas."

Since, Rodriguez has designed for the Tropicana, Caesar's Palace, Commerce Casino, the Crown Plaza Hotel, and the Dunes "Oasis." In Reno, Nevada, he developed the Circus Circus 12-storey clown pylon and grand façade for the Eldorado Hotel-Casino. He has created major concepts and images for numerous retail establishments, restaurants, wineries, and entertainment companies. He continues to provide conceptual work for Landmark Entertainment theme parks, Creative Retailing store interiors, the Hilton Hotel chain, and Ferrari-Carano Vineyards and Winery. He designed the opening stage set for the World's Fair in New Orleans, served as Art Director for Philadelphia's "We the People 2,000" United States' Bicentennial Parade, and as Consultant to the Olympic Games in Los Angeles. His illuminated designs can be found in Korea, Taiwan (Republic of China), and Thailand. More recently, he served as key production designer for "Walt Disney's Parade of Dreams," the parade celebrating Disneyland's 50th anniversary.

Now acclaimed by colleagues as "Float Designer Extraordinaire," Rodriguez has won more awards than any other designer in the history of the Rose Parade. He lives in the beautiful Windsor Square area of Hancock Park that he fell in love with as a youth. The neighborhood is one of LA's oldest, and is designated as an historic area. His home was built in 1919 by the president of the Bank of Milan; Raul is the fourth owner.

"Vinton Anderson, the original owner of what is now Fiesta Floats, was a mentor to me. As a boy I had the pleasure of meeting Isabella Coleman, and she has always been a great inspiration. I was privileged to design the float that won the first award given in her honor." He has ridden floats in the parade for 25 years, accompanied for 21 of those by his beloved Roxie. Roxie is gone, now, but Sebastian has come to take over her responsibilities, and at age two is already a parade veteran. Through the years Raul has designed for and collaborated with Fiesta Parade Floats, Charisma Floats, Festival Artists, Phoenix Decorating, American Decorating, Bravo, and Studio Concepts. He celebrates a network of friends that include other designers and builders, and extends to entertainers, celebrities, and clients on other continents. Many are lifelong friends. "I am one of the few private citizens to own a Muppet," he says. "Miss Piggy." He has a "close" family of 200-plus relatives, and he reaches out to inspire and mentor students from elementary school through college. He has established a scholarship founda-tion at California State University, Long Beach. "The school has one of the top art departments in the world, and the faculty selects my scholarship winners," he says with confidence. To encourage younger children, Raul has collaborated with YES!, the Young Entrepreneurs Society, illustrating text the children composed to celebrate the millennium Rose Parade. *Millenium Mischief/Posie Visits the Rose Parade* was published at the turn of the century, and underscores the values of courage, respect, and responsibility as well as creativity.

An elementary school textbook called *Pageants*, published by Houghton Mifflin in 1986, includes a chapter on the Tournament of Roses and an article about Raul. He smiles with gentle satisfaction when he relates the following story:

"One of my little cousins was using the book in class and saw my picture. 'That's my cousin Raul!' he exclaimed with excitement. The other children refused to believe him. When I found out about this, I arranged to visit the school with Roxie and do a presentation about art and float design. During the presentation, I called my little cousin up in front to assist me, and made sure that everyone knew that in fact he had been telling the truth."

Raul Rodriguez has achieved both fame and success, but he has not forgotten what's important. He has remarkable insight and integrity. "My father once told me, 'Do your work with honesty, intelligence, and diligence.

Floats begin in the imagination of designer's like Raul Rodriguez who shows the drawing for this float featuring pandas.

Next the drawing is mocked up as a 3-D maquette.

The sculpted-in-steel "wire frames" are assembled on the float chasis and wire mesh and foam are attached, painted and ready to receive flowers. Finally the float emerges complete on parade day with the help of volunteers.

These photos of the float building process are all by Jim Moore.

And sign your name proudly,' and I have tried always to follow that advice." In 2005, he and Sebastian proudly rode on the City of Whittier's float, reminding all who know Raul's story about the beginnings of his association with the Rose Parade.

Jim Moore is a professional photographer who became interested in Rose Parade float design and construction about 14 years ago. "It's like watching an autopsy in reverse," he comments, referring to the construction process. "A float barn is the world's biggest artist's loft." Jim visits Phoenix Decorating Company's facility often during each year, using black and white film that captures the artists during moments of intense concentration as they bend and weld and screen the steel skeletons of what will become lively animals, graceful arbors, and historic scenes. Jim has shared several of his beautiful pictures with us in this book. They convey the artistry behind the flowers in quiet, but profound depth.

Bill Lofthouse, founder and CEO of Phoenix Decorating Company, met Isabella Coleman when he was a 16 year-old applicant for a position with her float-building company. (He also met there a young employee named Gretchen, who would eventually become his wife.) After personnel manager Jim-

my Iwanaga hired him as a float driver, Bill became Coleman's "chief cook and bottle washer," chauffeuring her from place to place in her rusted-out Ford. "You could see the street beneath your feet," he laughs. To work for Isabella, one had first to find a part-time job elsewhere, so Bill became a painter and continued that line of work for 25 years or so, working on floats evenings and weekends.

"Isabella Coleman had a distinct design style," Bill often remarks; "She liked dragons and drippies." He points to a display of current float designs that feature long strands of flowers suspended from latticed trellises and overhangs. "Some of our floats still use that style, while others are very different." On the conference room wall is a framed

drawing of the Helms Bakeries float from 1960: "This float was Isabella's design. I rode under the front end as an observer." Next to it hangs another of Isabella's drawings. The similarity of style is clear.

The old drawings are just a taste of Bill's collection of Tournament artifacts. He and Gretchen collected antiques up until she passed away in 2004, and among their treasures are old silver trophy cups from early tournament days. Bill found the huge silver Isabella Coleman trophy tarnishing away in an old antique store and rescued it to the tune of $16,000. He and Gretchen donated it to the Tournament, and it now resides in a place of honor on the first landing of the central staircase at the Tournament House.

In addition to Tournament memorabilia and the plethora of paperwork that comes with running a huge business, Bill's office is packed with a variety of plaques that testify to years of community service. Elected to the International Festivals and Event Association (IFEA) Hall of Fame in 2004, he is a founding member and president of the California Festivals and Events Asso-

The coveted (and LARGE) Isabellla Coleman trophy.

ciation (CalFest) and past president of the IFEA. He is a city council-man in Bradbury, California. He has been involved for years with the American Cancer Society, the Pasadena Athletic Association, Optimist International Club, the University Club of Pasadena, and was instrumental in revitalizing the Pasadena YMCA. The Arcadia Methodist Hospital Foundation presented an award for distinguished service to Gretchen and Bill in 2001, and Bill will serve as chair of the Foundation in 2005. "Volunteering is important," he remarks. "You don't pick up business from it, but you establish relationships. Working with your hospital and the doctors, for example, means that they will remember who helped them when facilities are crowded and they're short-staffed and you need their help. It's just good sense to contribute to your community."

Phoenix, the largest of the float-building companies, has sent over 450 units down Colorado Boulevard. The company is the last of its kind remaining within the Pasadena city limits; all of its operations take place at two facilities, each situated within minutes of the parade route and Tournament Headquarters. Bill is often asked what has changed the most about the business over the years, and his answer is emphatic: "The cost of insurance." Each float builder is required to carry coverage on an occurrence basis for a minimum limit of $2,000,000 per float (or $5,000,000 in total for builders with three or more floats) and commercial automobile liability coverage for a minimum limit of $1,000,000 to include all owned, hired, and non-hired vehicles. Workers' Compensation insurance must cover employees and volunteers.

Bill has turned most of the company's operations over to his son Chris, who is the president of the company. Now in his forties, Chris was "born into the business." He grew up in Pasadena and found his passion in floatbuilding. Chris also found his wife in the business — she was working for his dad when he met her. His experience includes the Coca Cola® 110th Anniversary Celebration, the Orange Bowl Parade, the Kentucky Derby Festival, the Indianapolis 500 Festival Parade, and the National Day celebration in Singapore. Those experiences have taught him to appreciate the organization and precision of the Tournament organization, unequaled anywhere on the planet.

Chris's sister Michelle Lofthouse is the lead illustrator for the company. She holds a degree in music from the University of Delaware and teaches music in public schools, but she shares the family Rose Parade passion and has been designing floats since 1980. She works with a six-person creative team which has captured the Tournament's Extraordinaire Award for eleven straight years. "We call ourselves The First Family of Floatbuilding," their dad remarks. He pronounces the words seriously, with a tone of commitment and pride.

Above, Owners of Phoenix Decorating, Bill Lofthouse (left) with son Chris (right).

Opposite, this bent-steel fantasy will become an enchanted forest.

Driver's compartments have changed a bit since Chuck Rubsamen drove in 1941. This float cockpit is from 1993.

RUBBER NECKING?

In 1940, floats were built on truck chassis. Because of the artistic considerations of presenting a float, the low point of the design was front, and the high point in the rear. Thus, the high point was the engine.

That year, I was helping decorate a float. The driver for that float did not show up at parade time, so I was asked to drive the float! Sitting on a wood box, I put the engine in reverse and backed this float the length of the parade route. A fellow stood over me, and looking through the greenery, told me when to turn or stop, go faster or slower.

I would glance over my shoulder to judge the clearance on the sides while I looked down to keep the "pink line" in the center of the float.

I received a Rose Bowl ticket for my efforts. I was afraid I might have to view the game looking over my shoulder, as my muscles were almost frozen in that position.

(Stanford beat Nebraska 21 – 13 in the January 1, 1941 game.)

—Chuck Rubsamen

Chris echoes his dad's attitude: "You'll sense deep pride as you talk to us. The pressure is intense here: there's no such thing as extending the due date, and failure is unacceptable. But the rewards are incredible." He also comments about the high cost of insurance. While the Tournament is responsible for the parade, each company is completely responsible for the floats it builds, including insurance costs. "The easiest thing we do here is build the floats. We're really a steel fabrication shop. Each float is a prototype, and we build them from the bottom up. It's all about strength, sculpture, and structure. We're experts at hydraulics, mechanics, mega-sound systems, and computer systems that run complicated animations. But the headaches come from insurance liability and the pressure of deadlines."

Rising insurance costs aren't the only complication. The cost of steel went up 60% in 2004, which makes visitors better appreciate the racks of 20-foot lengths of quarter- and three-quarter-inch pencil steel along the wall. About 600 tons of steel are used each year in creating the chassis, basic structure, and sculpted figures for the 25 or so floats Phoenix builds. (The business purchases materials and special parts assemblies such as hydraulic lifts that can be recycled over and over again. These costs are amortized by the business, which saves on clients' costs.)

The company's annual shopping list is daunting. Over 70,000 square feet of plywood form float bases, platforms, and staircases. 225,000 square feet of chicken wire form large areas for floral decoration. 350,000 square feet of aluminum screening are used to cover detailed areas of sculpted figures and serve as a base for pasted dry flowers and dry decoration. 14 tons of plastic foam are used as a base to hold water-filled plastic vials into which fragile flowers such as individual roses and orchids are inserted. In 2004, Phoenix used more than 700,000 of those vials! About 8,000 gallons of various glues are used each year: "flora glue" for whole fresh flowers, leaves, and grass; "sticky glue" for flower petals; "white glue" for seeds, grains, and other dry materials; and "spray adhesive" for areas featuring spices and powdered dry materials. 16 tons of those dry materials create broad areas of color and fine detailing on sculpted figures. 20 million or so flowers include about 400,000 roses and 550,000 carnations. Stadium concert-quality speakers provide up to 30,000 watts of sound, a Phoenix specialty. (Parade viewers should try to spot the huge speaker screens, strategically placed behind large floral sprays anchored in maché tubs.)

The Tournament Float Manual contains all of the specifications to which builders must adhere. The Manual is the product of many years' experience, and is designed to help prevent accident and injury to participants and viewers alike. Typical float size is 55 feet in length, 17 feet 4 inches in height, and 18 feet in width. The reason for the anomalous height limit is that all floats must pass under the Sierra

Tim Estes, president of Fiesta Parade Floats, shows off some of the steel armatures that will become parts of a float.

Above, the cockpit of a float under construction at Charisma Floats.
Left, Larry Crain, owner of Charisma shows models of floats being built in his shop.
Below, Larry Crain checks the progress of the float props.

Dragons, knights, and castles are always crowd pleasers, like these from Farmer's Insurance Group.

Madre freeway bridge, which is 17 feet 8 inches high. Any float that will extend and retract after passage under the bridge must be able to do so within 60 seconds in order to maximize the entertainment value for the parade audience.

Safety is paramount. All float passengers are seat-belted in. When the float undergoes the last of three Tournament inspections, a fire drill is held to ascertain that all will be safe no matter what might go awry.

Work on floats begins shortly after the first of each year. At any given time, five to seven floats occupy the floor of the Raymond Avenue facility. Chris works with each float's designer to guide the logistics of the building process. The designs are, of course, drawn to scale, and the factory floors are gridded with white paint at 1-foot intervals so that assemblies can be built to specification.

Once a float design is approved by a client and converted to mechanical drawings, the company obtains the necessary truck components and configures the chassis. The float's wheelbase, the distance from the centerline of the steering axle to the centerline of the rear or drive axle, must be at least 33% of the total length of the float. No more than 40% of the total float length may be in front of the front steering axle, or behind the rear driving axle.

The engines used to drive the floats are geared low to prevent overheating while traveling at 2½ miles per hour along the five-mile

route. "Gearing is the key," instructs Chris. "In the old days they used junk car motors. Now we use new or rebuilt engines and make sure that they run optimally to keep pollution down." The gear ratio of the float must be chosen so that the driver does not have to ride the brakes in order to maintain parade speed, and so that the engine RPMs are maintained at a level adequate for optimal cooling and charging operations. To minimize the possibility of vapor lock, fuel tanks must be bottom draw. The skirts of each float hide multiple fans and carefully regulated venting systems to fight engine heat and protect the crew from exhaust fumes. Each float must be equipped with a permanently installed towing connection point and a removable towbar. Initial road testing is done as early as May.

Tires are a major issue. "Flat tires on floats are not fun!" Chris admonishes. A float can weigh up to 50,000 pounds, all of which rests on its tires. Most tires used today are either filled with a solid foam rubber component or made of solid fork-lift-type rubber in order to support the weight of the float, which increases critically if (rarely, thank goodness) rain soaks the float. The float frame and skirts must have a minimum ground clearance of eight inches.

Animation is a Phoenix specialty, and is the most costly budget item after insurance. The

Things can, and occasionally do go wrong. In 1983 the IHOP (International House of Pancakes) float caught fire during the parade.

Animation, such as with this moving dinosaur, brings even more excitement to the floats.

easy jobs turn wheels, flap wings, and wink eyes. More complicated systems might run multiple fountains, blast out "steam," operate a giant calliope, or swivel the hips of a giant figure. Each movement happens thanks to a network of tubes and hydraulic gizmos that has been dreamed up, machined, assembled, tested, and re-tested by the crew.

Pencil steel is shaped around a rod-bending tree or tire and placed on the floor grid to create exactly the sculpture of the float. "Very few people create in this art form," Chris notes, nodding toward an artist clad in overalls and a welder's mask. The steel is then covered with aluminum screen wire, using special glue. Bob Dickey's Coral Industries has developed special glues just for the parade, and had to obtain a special exemption from Air Quality Management District for its use.

Next, cocooning urethane foam is applied with a spray applicator. This all-purpose coating allows for many special effects, from water systems to fireworks. Maché pots nestle in the coated flanks of the float, ready for soaked Oasis® florist foam and beautiful flowers. Handrails and cabin posts are wrapped in foam pipe insulation, then ironed and dented to make them look like hewn wood. Special effects can range from water fountains, to propane torches, even fireworks. Says Chris, "This is show biz!"

Phoenix is the largest buyer of flowers for the Rose Parade. Because of the size of its floral

needs, the company has its own growers.

99% of the time, floats are manned by two operators. The driver is hidden at the rear. He or she drives "blind," responding to instructions delivered via hardwired headsets. The observer is hidden toward the front of the float and mans a set of redundant power-assisted brakes capable of stopping the float against the engine in case of emergency. He or she must be able to see the front edges of the float as well as have good visibility of the parade route, both down the street and immediately in front of the

"This is show biz!"
——Chris Lofthouse

float. The observer "steers" the driver with words, peering out through camouflaged screening. The driver and the observer have to be a compatible, well-coordinated team. Says Chris, "I like to recruit them in pairs, often husbands and wives or girlfriends and boyfriends."
Sometimes as many as five additional operators hide in the body of the float, manning hydraulic systems, water systems, and electric generators that run the float's animation. Even in floats pulled by horses such as the Budwiser Clydesdales, there is almost always an engine that helps with maneuvering and overcoming initial inertia to help the animals get the float started.

All crew areas must have a seat, controls that are clearly la-

beled, and a storage area for personal items, including drinking water. One crew member must have an audible emergency signaling device. Crew areas must be protected from high temperatures and carbon monoxide: no compartment is permitted to reach a temperature higher than 120°.

By June of each year, many Phoenix floats have already advanced through their entire construction stage, passed Tournament safety testing, been color-coded by the creative art department staff, and await only flowers and glue to be parade ready. They are moved to a separate location to make room for the construction, sculpting, cocooning, foaming, and coloration of another group of floats. By the end of late November, all of the floats are ready for dry decoration, where hundreds of materials that will not wilt are applied. Then comes that wonderfully hectic phase where 16,000 volunteers apply the fresh flowers.

Tim Estes CFEE (Certified Festival & Events Executive) has been involved with Rose Parade floats since he was eight years old, starting out as a float decorator. Since 1988, Tim has been President of Fiesta Parade Floats and, along with Jim Hynd AIFD (American Institute of Floral Designers), Fiesta's Vice President

A special glue is applied . . .

In an assembly-line, three-step process, stems are clipped off of leaves . . .

And, the still sticky leaves are pressed onto the float in an overlapping pattern.

Smaller volunteers often get tapped to climb into the tight spots and decorate virtually every inch of the floats' surfaces.

Coleslaw anyone? These whole purple cabbages will find themselves impaled and stuck to a float before the night is over.

Names taped on the back of volunteer workers facilitates communications when hundreds of strangers come together to decorate the floats. They often leave as lasting friends.

One voulunteer paints white glue on to the color coded area, while another tosses and pats the correct color materials in place behind her.

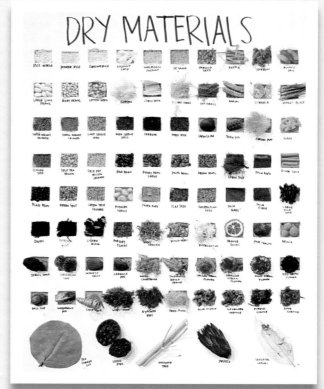

This complex chart shows volunteers what materials are what colors so they can follow the "paint-by-number" float plans.

These young girls share a laugh while working on a float.

Volunteers use tweezers to pick out stray, colored petals from a white rice background. It's actually that meticulous!

Members of the Petal Pushers volunteer group work at preparing blossoms. This group volunteers on many floats to earn money for financing their own Lutheran Hour Ministries float. Many Petal Pushers come back year after year.

and Floral Director, has created the second-largest float company producing floats for the annual Rose Parade. Fiesta is located just east of Pasadena in the City of Duarte. The company has achieved the highest prize-winning rate for the parade, 67%, and has won the Sweepstakes Award a record 11 years in a row for the 1994 through the 2004 Rose Parades.

Tim started working full-time in the industry when he was 16. His father was an engineer who built spacecraft parts for over 30 years at the Jet Propulsion Laboratory (JPL) in Pasadena, and Tim inherited his father's knack for solving engineering problems. "I've always been fascinated with the parade and how the floats are built," Tim comments. "The Rose Parade is a labor of love and a pleasure to participate in." He converses about the physics behind float construction casually; gear ratios, animation systems and mathematical formulas that have become second nature over years of experience spill effortlessly into normal conversation.

"This business has three facets: sales, working with people, and creativity. I love all three. It's not a big money-maker, but I do it for that euphoric feeling I get when something we have built goes down the street and makes people smile. The Rose Parade is a 'time out' for people. It allows them to forget their problems for a few hours. That's important to me."

First-time visitors seem to ask Tim a number of the same questions; one that usually comes up is, "Which has been your favorite float of all?"

"I can't tell you which is my favorite or which is the best — the floats are like my children and I am proud of all of them. I guess that you could say, though, that I'm especially partial to the ones that people thought could not be built or couldn't work." Making floats work is Tim's passion. He's a quiet guy, kind of serious, but has to grin when he recalls surprising officials with designs that not only worked, but won awards to boot.

> **"I can't tell you which is my favorite or which is the best — the floats are like my children and I am proud of all of them."**
> —— Tim Estes

"We built a float for Lawry's back in 1987. I was 31 years old then, working as the foreman for Fiesta Floats. It was a standard 55-foot float float, but it was unusual. It portrayed Garfield riding on a 3-wheeled motorcycle. The wheels were ten feet tall, and the front wheel actually steered the float while the two rear wheels drove the float. The Tournament officials were worried that it wouldn't work."

The engine for that float was a Chevy 350 V-8, but the important issue was that the 10-foot wheels had to turn at a certain number of revolutions per minute (RPM). Normal parade speed is 2.5 miles per hour, which is 220-feet per minute. Since the 10-foot wheel travels about 31.4 feet per revolution, the wheel would need to "roll" at 7 RPM to travel at normal parade speed. Tim was hoping to keep the engine RPM between 800 and 900 RPM. Thus, the engine RPM (800 to 900) divided by the desired wheel RPM (7), would require a gear reduction in the range of 121 to 1 (850 divided by 7) to achieve the desired parade speed.

As money is always a budget issue, Tim searched the float yard for available parts that could be used. Tim used the automatic transmission that was with the Chevy engine along with two in-line transfer cases from trucks, which are a type of transmission. After the second transfer case, the driveshaft drove an altered truck axle placed about 6 feet above the ground, inside the float. From the two sides of the altered truck axle, a custom built "half shaft" then delivered power to a heavy duty sprocket which used a heavy duty roller chain for a final chain drive reduction of 4 to 1 at the big wheels. Overall, Tim's system had a 118 to 1 gear reduction, which accomplished the goal of making the float work and used existing parts

for the unique system to save on money. Says he, "Floats are like building your own Tonka Toy Truck — but in a much larger scale."

As it turned out, not only did the float work beautifully, it solved a parade convoy emergency. Tournament rules mandate that floats be towed to the Parade Formation Area on South Orange Grove in Pasadena. In the early hours on parade day, while traveling up the steep hill of Fair Oaks Avenue in South Pasadena, the tow truck pulling Garfield and his bike broke down. "Power up the float," Tim commanded, and the float proceeded up the hill under its own power, pushing the tow vehicle up the hill as well!

"Southern California Edison participated in the Rose Parade for a number of years and presented me with an engineering challenge," he continues. "They asked that their floats be completely powered by electricity, using batteries." Edison want-

ed to use the same electric motor and battery pack that it had on some of its own battery-powered vehicles. The problems with that turned out to be battery pack weight and bulk. One battery pack weighed more than 3,300 pounds and measured about 5 feet by 6 feet in size, and the float needed three of them if the desired back-up systems were to be maintained. Tim built the chassis to incorporate the huge battery packs, which powered not only the engine, but also the power steering and power brakes. "We used 12-volt DC-operated vacuum pumps for the vacuum needed for the brakes, and connected an automobile power steering pump with a fan belt to another DC motor to operate the power steering. To drive the float they required two independent electric motors. The high speed/high torque motors were connected to truck transfer cases, which in turn, drove a common drive shaft using sprockets and heavy duty roller chains, which turned the drive shaft to the rear axle."

Tim grins as he recalls Edison's Vice President Lou Phelps's concern before the first test drive. "Is this going to work?" Lou queried.

Tim tried to keep from chuckling. "I don't know," he replied, observing Lou's stricken expression. Tim did know — he had test-driven the float himself the night before, but wanted to see Lou's reaction. Once the float moved, they both broke out in laughter and Lou heaved a sigh of relief.

1988 was Tim's first year as the owner of Fiesta Parade Floats. At that time the floats were kept in a huge tent. On December 8 the Santa Ana winds tore through town, gusting over 100 miles per hour, and the tent came crashing down on top of the floats. "We worked 24 hours a day under rented lighting to get them re-built and ready in time for the parade," he recalls, shaking his head. "That is not what I had in mind for my first year in business."

Tim's wife Martha rode on the FTD float that year, as she often does. While she waited on the float in her costume for the parade to start, an envious spectator commented to her, "You're so lucky to ride! How did you manage to get to do it?"

"I went to bed with the owner," Martha replied with a

smile and a laugh. As everybody in the business points out, float building tends to be a family affair.

It is not, however, a business for financial cowards. Tim's company employs about 30 people full time, year-round, which is a tremendous financial burden, along with numerous items of high expense. For example, a new float chassis costs about $40,000, including a rebuilt engine, a specially prepared transmission that includes a high-stall torque converter, manual shift body and heavy-duty clutches. Chassis can be re-used, but only last eight to ten years before metal fatigue begins to set in. It takes an average of 7,000 person/hours to decorate one float, including cleaning the flower vials in bleach water, trimming the flowers, putting each stem in a vial, and applying them to the float. All volunteers must be covered with Worker's Compensation insurance, which runs about $15,000 for the month of December. Lots of organizations, such as the Girl Scouts, send teams of volunteers, in return for which the float builders make a donation to the organization. This is handled through a contract. "We can't count on volunteers' just showing up," Tim notes. "We need to have a secure commitment." Once volunteers get a taste of float building, they tend to return year after year. One such couple is Joe and Gwen Hughes, a retired couple from Texas, who arrive each year in their motor home and stay for four to six weeks. "It gets in your blood," Tim says. "There's a special camaraderie amongst the decorators, especially the kids, that comes from working on a beautiful project with a common goal."

The last time Tim actually drove in a parade was in 1976. Since then, he has had too much supervision to do to be hidden away in a compartment under a float's skirts. "I do hold the world's record for float-driving speed, though," he grins. It seems that a Fiesta float driver also worked at Irwindale Speedway and came up with the notion of taking a float to the Irwindale racetrack and opening up the throttle. The idea was shared with Doug Stokes at the raceway and he loved the idea. Floats are generally built to go no more than twice the normal parade speed, which would be 5 miles per hour, with the axles welded in solid meaning they have no suspension to aid in turning. That float reached the incredible speed of 16 miles per hour. The following year, Doug suggested that an attempt be made to break the record. This time Tim felt he should be at the controls and drove the City of Duarte float at the same track, setting a new record of just over 37 miles per hour. The float had to slow down for the turns, but going down the straight-aways the float was exceeding 48 miles per hour.

Tim loves getting kids involved in the parade. One year, for example, kids from the Make a Wish Foundation were to ride on the Elks Club float. "A sweet little girl came to be on the float the night

The Kodak float "steams" up the parade route in the 2004 parade.

Young volunteers climb scaffolding to put the finishing touches on this giant sea maiden. Below, volunteers from seven to 87 spend an unforgettable New Year's Eve working together to create the magic we all can't wait to see every New Year's morning.

Details on the floats create some spectacular flower arrangements in their own right, such this unusual combination of long stem apricot colored roses and dried grasses. Below, these vialed rose-buds are color coded and numbered to tell workers where on the float they belong.

before the parade during the judging at the building site," he recalls quietly. "She smiled and had a great time. Unfortunately, she wasn't able to make it to the Parade itself, but she was the Queen of the float while she was on the float the night before."

The theme for the 1995 Parade was "Sports . . . Quest For Excellence". For the FTD float, the design showcased two 30-foot Italian gondolas racing. About a month before the parade, TV commentator Bob Eubanks stopped by to visit with Tim and had a favor to ask. One of Bob's sons was a fireman, and he had a firefighter friend whose daughter was going through difficult chemotherapy treatment that left her without any hair. Bob wanted to know if there was any way she could ride a float in the upcoming Rose Parade. Without a hesitation, the answer was YES. Tim talked to her parents and informed them that his wife Martha, who is a nurse, would also ride on the float and could watch over the child during the parade. The costume people gave the little girl a beautiful costume that included a velvet headband with a large jewel on it to partially cover up her head. She "had a blast" riding on the float and waving to the people in the crowd. It was her day. Bob had the TV camera folks zoom in on her during the parade, but no comment was made about her illness. The sole intent was to give a little girl the ride of her life and a moment she and her parents would never forget.

Tim's face grew serious at first when we asked him if he could tell us any humorous anecdotes about the perils of float production. "Well, things happen," he said. "You just have to go with the flow." Then his eyes began to twinkle. " I can tell you a couple of things that happened over 30 years ago, far enough back that I won't hurt anyone's feelings by telling about them."

It seems that, back in those days, floats had a problem getting enough fresh air to the driver's compartment. A float builder decided to build in a duct system connected to extremely powerful fans to blow fresh air onto the driver. The fans worked beautifully, except that they sucked in pieces of floral debris and horse droppings from the street below, pelting the driver in the face. The driver was not happy with the newest invention.

On another occasion, a lovely young lady was asked to ride on a float dressed as a Southern belle. Her perch was positioned directly above the driver's compartment. Her beautiful hoop skirt was connected to the float and decorated with lovely flowers. Once belted in, she was unable to leave her position for any reason. Unfortunately, the poor girl had forgotten the advice about not drinking water before the parade, and found herself in dire straits toward the end of the route. The unfortunate driver suffered the consequences, and the splattered engine beside him produced an unusual type of steam for a moment or two.

One of the most memorable persons associated with Rose Parade float-building is Jim Femino, now a venerable Fiesta employee. He sits quietly at a bench in the Fiesta barn, surrounded by lengths of pencil steel and the skeleton frames of dolphins and birds what will be bluebells and lilies of the valley on a lovely parade float. His hands are gnarled with hard work and arthritis, but he wields a simple hand tool deftly, shaping a straight steel rod into a graceful curve to match a template drawn on a piece of plywood with black felt marker. He has made 76 of the belled flowers so far for this one float.

Jim has been associated with the Rose Parade since he first began as a float driver in 1949. He looks like a character from an old black and white Western, and indeed he has played many small parts as gangsters and "heavies" in Hollywood movies. In the Rodney Dangerfield movie *The Fourth Tenor*, Jim plays the shoeshine man in front of the bakery. "I'm a pretty nice guy," Jim will assure you if you visit him at Fiesta, especially if you're female. He writes screenplays in his spare time, and has sold some. He is also a licensed farrier. In the 1960s he invented a device to fix horses' cracked hooves, which saved them from euthanasia.

Jim first met Tim Estes when Tim was 12 years old. They share a vivid memory of working on a float together back in 1972 or so. The Parade theme that year had to do with movies, and Jim was building a float modeled after the Bogart/Hepburn film's *African Queen*. Tim could scaffold a float by himself by then. The float's model of the African Queen was covered in white flowers. No sooner had the flowers been applied than it began to rain — and rain — and rain. All of the beautiful white flower petals turned a drab shade of brown. "Take a square shovel and scrape all of those flowers off the boat!" Jim commanded, as Tim's jaw dropped in astonishment. Tim did as he was told, and the team worked all night long to replace the ruined flowers with new ones. Alan Ladd's widow Sue and Edith Head were float judges that year. Because the Queen float was also decorated with red roses, they awarded it the Rose prize. Jim claims that all of "his" floats were banner floats.

A third float-building company is Charisma Floats, located in Azusa. Larry Crain is the President and Owner of the company. Jim Hynd was Larry's mentor when Larry first broke into the business. "He and Raul set the standard 20 years ago," he comments with respect. Larry's clear about his comparative expertise: "I'm not a mechanic or a welder. I come from a public relations and marketing background." He has a degree in music education, and a background in sales, specifically medical supplies. He and his wife Betty attend Bethany Baptist Church, and became involved in

Expert steel wire sculptor, Jim Femino, of Fiesta Floats, then bends then welds the pencil steel in the shapes and forms that will become animals and plants and figures.

float decoration as a fundraiser. Eventually he asked to be considered as a float supervisor for the old Fiesta Float Company, which is now Fiesta Parade Floats. Charisma Floats was started by a couple who asked Larry to join their company when Fiesta changed its name and ownership. Larry purchased Charisma from that couple about 14 years ago. Says he, "We decorate similarly to the other companies, but our emphasis is more floral. There is no 'float school.' All of the float builders came from a volunteer background." His company usually constructs between two and five parade entries each year.

"The first thing float builders do at the beginning of each new year is to prepare for Theme Draft Day. The theme for the next parade is released in mid-January. Designers have until the second week of February to meet with clients and come up with 8 ½ inch by 11 inch pencil sketches and float names that relate to the theme. Entrants draw numbers to submit two drafts per float.

In Round 1 of the drawing, we submit drafts 1 through 10. In Round 2 of the drawing, we submit drafts 11 through 20. The Tournament President and his committee members view the designs for each round. We go in with more designs than we will register. Even so, several hundred designs are registered overall."

Charisma's designs are done by Raul Rodriguez. Sponsors apply for parade entry a year and a half in advance. Once accepted, they have until the end of February to confirm. Positions for additional applicants do not open up until March. If a submission has not been sold by May 1, other designers can use the concept. A favorite client for Charisma for five years was the country of Malaysia. Larry would go there to get his designs approved by the Minister of Tourism. Their floats were always large, and 50 to 60 feet tall. If a rider were positioned 20 feet high on the float, the 45-second fire exit rule proved challenging. Larry's designers called for the use of fire ladders to provide quick exits through windows. The design had to meet cultural requirements, and all costumes had to be accurate. The float's passengers would wear costumes similar to those depicted on the float itself. Larry eventually helped the Malaysians start their own parade in Kuala Lumpur.

Charisma's float builders are very careful to avoid the possibility of a float's breaking down and needing to be towed away from the parade. "No one likes breakdowns. I remember that Bob Hope was riding in a Chrysler that broke down in one parade."

Joe Lonergan recalls the incident:

"It was Tige Payne's year as President of the Tournament of Roses. He had selected Bob Hope as the Grand Marshal. I was on the Parade Operations Committee and was assigned to the Colorado and Sierra Madre Boulevard area.

"As the parade approached, my HAM radio operator (cell phones were far in the future) reported that Bob Hope's "beautiful Chrysler convertible" had a dead battery, and headquarters wanted us to push his "beautiful Chrysler convertible" until they could get a fresh battery to the car. I dutifully jumped into my Jeep and explained the problem to the driver, and we were off.

"We drove a block or two to the west and pulled in behind Hope's "beautiful Chrysler convertible," which was being pushed by six tired-looking youths. I told them to step aside so that we could push Mr. Hope, his wife, and his "beautiful Chrysler convertible." Hope was waving and smiling at the crowd when he motioned for me to approach him. Continuing to wave and smile, he said

through his teeth, "Get that damned Jeep out of here!" and signaled to the young men to continue pushing.

"The television cameras were set up at Colorado and Sierra Madre Boulevard, and he was not about to have his sponsor Chrysler embarrassed by having that "beautiful Chrysler convertible" pushed by a lowly Jeep.

"Of course, a few years later Chrysler purchased Jeep, but that wasn't the case in 1969."

Larry Crain notes that the Tournament Association fines floatbuilders if a float breaks down during the parade, although builders can appeal the fine through a review board. American Automobile Association is the official tow company that's on call during the parade.

Float-building provides plenty of opportunities for things to go wrong. Fire is always a liability. Pampas grass and raffia are the two most flammable plant materials used by decorators. A special variance allows the use of fire retardant on these materials. Colors are critically important, and weather or disease can affect shipments of flowers.

In 1934, 12.86 inches of rain fell in Pasadena during the 48 hours before the Tournament. Streets were flooded, and so was the Rose Bowl. Forty people died, some of them washed from their cars, some swept into storm drains, and others crushed by mud and rock slides. Ironically, the theme that year was "Tales of

the Seven Seas" and the Grand Marshal was U. S. Navy Admiral William Sims. Since 1935, no parade theme has alluded to water.

Red is a popular, but difficult color for float decoration. Besides red roses, decorators typically use whole carnations, carnation petals, or poinsettia leaves. "Several years ago, there was a mum disease that really caused a problem for us, Crain recalls. When decorators popped the mum head off of a stem, the entire blossom shattered to pieces. We had four floats to decorate that year, and every one of them was to be done with white mums. We ordered more mums, but some of them were white with white centers, some were white with yellow centers, and some were white with green centers. One of the floats ended up with a horse that had a strange kind of stripe down one of its legs,." Another year, an order for $5,000 worth of carnations from Columbia never arrived. A replacement shipment had to be rushed through a flower broker. Sometimes float materials are ordered with the environment in mind. "Forests should have between 30 and 50 trees per acre to stay healthy," says Larry. "The sap in healthy trees kills bark beetles. For the *Three Tenors* float, we gathered bark from the forests to help with cleanup."

Decoration Week is exciting for Larry because of his interaction with youthful volunteers. "Sometimes the kids who come to work arrive without a goal or purpose in life. I start by compli-

RAIN OR SHINE . . . THE PARADE GOES ON

The Pasadena Tournament of Roses Parade has never been canceled due to rain. It has rained on the Parade in: 1895, the year that the Tournament of Roses Association was formed; 1899, when the start of the Parade was delayed to 3:45 p.m.; 1906; 1910; 1916; 1922; 1934, the only year that the Parade had a theme associated with water; 1937; 1955; and in 2006.

Above, these two conceptual drawings of floats from the 1934 parade reflect the water theme of that year, and coincidentally, the weather.

In 2006 bad luck struck again, with a vengeance after 51 dry years. The parade day dawned gray and a slow drizzle gained momentum to become a downpour before parade's end. But the show must go on—the world was watching!

These two floats in 1934 represented the "water theme." Above, the float commemorates the Colorado River Aqueduct project that would bring water to southern California. Below, the float promotes Paramount Pictures 1934 movie Search for Beauty, starring Buster Crab and Ida Lupino. The movie had a sea theme.

menting them and thanking them. Over the week, their personalities seem to change. They don't miss a day! It's so much fun to watch! As the week progresses, the float becomes 'alive' and takes on its own personality. Once the kids have worked on a float, they OWN it. 'That's my float,' you'll hear them say, even if they only worked on one square foot of it." Larry understands and shares their emotional investment; he describes December 31st, the day the floats undergo final judging, thus: "It's emotional, like birthing a baby."

Larry gives careful instructions to the float passengers. "Make SURE that you don't eat or drink that morning! You're going to be on the float for five hours. You may not get off the float for any reason other than a fire alarm. If necessary, wear adult Pampers." He will tell you quietly, however, "On occasion, a float's flowers have been 'watered.' It doesn't seem to hurt them much." Riders are required to be on location by 5:30 a.m. Sometimes they have to ride to their lofty perches on a forklift.

After the parade, says Larry, "The birds take over. They love millet, which is a popular decorating material. Rice isn't good for them, and needs to be removed from floats that will be stored outside for future recycling."

Not to be overlooked, by any means, are the floats that have been built by non-profit organizations. As costs of materials increase, these faithful entrants scramble to make ends meet and still meet their own high standards for their entries.

All sorts of fantastic creatures show up on Tournament of Roses floats, like this dolphin steed in 2005.

The California Polytechnical Universities' floats are the only ones designed, built, and financed entirely by students. Cal Poly got started in the parade early on. Donald E. Miller was an ornamental horticulture student and a resident of San Marino. His father was involved with the Tournament. One year, a float entrant dropped out of the parade in September. Don, without checking or consulting with anyone, grasped the opportunity and committed the university to entering a float. There were only 90 days remaining before New Year's Day. The student float builders made the deadline, but went over their $50 budget by $3.47 because they purchased lollipops to distribute to children along the parade route. A Mrs. Rimpaw paid the debt on their behalf.

Ronald R. Simons, Associate Vice President, worries that non-profits may eventually "bail" because of high costs. Cal Poly has been participating in the Tournament for over 57 years. As a student, Ron was a float chairperson for three years, and has continued his affiliation with the effort ever since, working on every float entered since 1960. "Most float builders budget between $150,000 and $200,000 per float.

The dolphin on the previous page is featured on this float from Smart and Final in 2005. The water theme jinx doesn't seem to hold true for individual floats! Below, this train float from Honda has the distinction of being the longest float ever to date in 2005.

This fantastical creation represents Kodak in 2005, and features "photos" of people that are rendered in flower petals and other vegetable matter. Below, a giant sized tribute to Bob Hope shows the entertainer reclining amid giant-sized memorabilia.

A third of that goes for production, another third for floral, and the remaining third for overhead. Our University currently needs about $45,000 to put a float in the parade. Our labor, of course, is free, but increasing fees for our students mean that more of them have to work part time while they go to school, which cuts into their volunteer time." The student float designers and builders, however, share a fiercely competitive spirit, and research creative ways to recycle their chassis and materials. The chassis was first designed as a senior project at Cal Poly San Luis Obispo. It was designed in two sections, held together with patterned bolting holes — no welding. It is hydrostatically driven by two primary power units and some pneumatics.

Cal Poly's parade entry stems from several organizations: the Rose Float Alumni Association shares its expertise with the Rose Float Club, which constantly recruits new student members. The Rose Float Committee handles legal sanctions and the float budget. "There is something for everybody in this project," Ron notes. "Our motto is 'Learn by Doing.' What better project could provide the opportunity?" Many of the university's graduates are now Tournament members. Many alumni continue to serve as float drivers and float builders. One woman has become a floral designer for the parade floats. "And we use the term 'Rose Float Marriage' around here," Ron laughs, "because so many couples have met during the project, fallen in love, and eventually married."

The Cal Poly float, a joint effort between Cal Poly Pomona and Cal Poly San Luis Obispo, begins with a concept design contest that is held as soon as the new theme becomes available. Cal Poly is the only consecutive school entry in the parade, and the University is proud of that status. The Art Design classes at both schools are given the theme as a class assignment: whatever they design must allow a viewer to grasp the theme connection in seconds, without audio support. No names appear on the entries, and voting rights represent both schools equally. Sometimes design elements from two or more entries may be combined.

"Employers love our graduates' 'No Fear' concept," he chuckles. Our grads know how to think through problems. The one's who have worked on floats tend to secure good jobs because of their engineering experience. I have watched introverted students blossom because of this work."

San Luis Obispo builds half of the chassis and base and drives it to the Pomona campus in November each year. The Pomona students attach it to their half and secure the characters and animation mechanisms. The float is then cocooned with latex foam, just as are the professionally-made floats. Thousands of students, alumni, and community members team together to decorate the float; many of the decorators started as students and have returned year after year.

Opposite, Disney enters a special float and show to commemorate the 50th Anniversary of the Disneyland theme park.

THE "HAPPIEST PLACE ON EARTH"

I became a member of the Tournament of Roses in 1963 at the age of 43. Six years and three committees later, I was assigned to provide entertainment at the Huntington Hotel for all of the float participants. Big job! The Walt Disney Corporation, with many of its world-loved characters, was to lead off the parade that year, and they solved my problem. We were offered the entire cast and show of Uncle Tom's Cabin, the number one show at Disneyland.

The night the show was presented at the Huntington, I arranged to feed the entire cast and managers from Disney with a full sit-down dinner in a special room. That, the Disney people announced, was a big success.

The next year, at the start of the Christmas season promotion called "Candlelight," my wife, our three children, and I were invited to a formal dinner with top officials of Disney and members of the Disney family.

That invitation has been extended to us for 20 years, and is the highlight of our Christmas kickoff.

—Byrd Christian

While up-sized everything is the trend in float building, these whales are merely life-sized!

Sometimes the characters on the floats just make you laugh.

Each parade float participant receives a VIP package that includes four parade tickets, grandstand seating for four people, tickets to the VIP luncheon, and game tickets. The college president sits with students on the parade route, and puts on a special dinner for the students involved.

"There are lots of stories I could share with you," Ron muses. "We used to have to drive our float from the campus to Pasadena. Now it has to be towed because of Tournament rules. It's always cold at night just before the parade, and it's always an adventure. Once our float hit a low-hanging power line at San Gabriel Boulevard and Huntington. Just imagine a big pink hippo wrapped around a power pole, which had to be removed in order to untangle the float! Once we had a blowout and had to steal a tire temporarily to get going again. We couldn't do that now; back then it was just considered a kind of prank. Another year, we did a roller coaster float, and didn't get the animation perfected until December 31st, the day before the parade. Another time, the rubber on our recycled tires came off, and our float left grooves in the asphalt all the way down the Boulevard. It was a tough trip home, especially when it began to rain. God bless the Pasadena police for their patience with us, and thank goodness that the Tournament puts up with us."

Another of Ron's favorite tales is about how one young man named Rick, many years ago, took advantage of a stop in the parade to run from the float to a nearby restaurant in order to use their facilities. It seems that the fellow was gone for an inordinately long time, and the Parade had begun moving. His friends on the Cal Poly float called out, "Hey, Rick!" When there was no immediate response, the band behind the float picked up the chant and called, "Hey, Rick!" over and over and over. Soon the crowd along the street joined the chorus. The chanting continued until the poor lad appeared. That was probably one of his life's most embarrassing moments.

One year when I was serving as Float Construction Chairman, I received a three o'clock-in-the-morning call at home from one of the float mechanics. It was raining, and the Cal Poly float had broken down in Irwindale on its way to the decorating site, just a day or two before the Parade. The rain was gradually washing its "paint by number" color scheme off into the gutters and the students were in despair. We called a tow truck, which towed them to the float barn and didn't charge them a cent for the service. Once the float arrived, the poor kids had to re-paint all of the colors so that the flowers could be applied correctly in time for the parade. That was a very long night for them.

Several cities enter floats in the parade. Torrance is one of those. Sidney Torrance, one of the founders of the Valley Hunt Club, lived in Pasadena and owned an oil field development in an unincorporated area, which he named Torrance. The first Torrance float, entered

Las Vegas enters a rare float in the 2005 Tournament of Roses to celebrate that city's 100th birthday. This float rider's radiant smile shows the fun-loving spirit of her city.

in 1914, displayed an oil rig. That year was the second and last time both a Queen and a King were chosen as officiating royalty for the Tournament. A picture in the Tournament archives shows the crowd watching the chariot races, with a blimp flying overhead. The Torrance float won a trophy, which was found in a pawn shop in 2001 by the Torrance City Manager. The next Torrance entry was in 1947. Since that time, the city has been a regular in the Parade. In 2005, Torrance entered its 51st Rose Parade float.

The current president of the Torrance Rose Float Association is Mary Hoffman, a first grade teacher by day. She has led the association for over nine years. "We do it because we love it," she says with a smile.

Jack Williams is the vice president of the association. His wife Ann Williams is in charge of the volunteers. Beginning in October of each year, Ann schedules some 700 shifts of volunteers for float decoration. "Using our own people makes a difference," she smiles. "Many other cities use Girl Scouts and the like to do the decorating. The City of Torrance gives money to the association, and we raise money, too. People pay $5 each to ride the buses. I put in five days of my own time decorating each year."

Jack retired from TRW. He has an interesting story to relate about the 2000 parade. Edison's float had a space theme. Hector de la Torre, the mayor of Southgate, was the liaison between Edison and the public. He had just been elected assemblyman. He wanted an astronaut to ride on the Edison float. He had tried to get a contact through NASA, but hadn't had any luck. He talked to Jack about it. Jack knows Dan Golden from TRW days, and called him. Golden arranged for astronaut Yvonne Cagle to ride on the float. Yvonne loved the experience, and still exclaims over being "treated like a queen." Her family was given a trip to Disneyland, and was transported by limousine on several occasions. She went to the float barn to meet Torrance High School seniors who were working on the float. Raul Rodriguez was there, and the two of them sat down for an hour with the kids to talk about career goals and objectives.

The Lutheran Hour is another non-profit organization that enters a float in the parade each year. The mission of the Lutheran Hour Float Committee is to "provide a Christian witness and a message of hope in Jesus Christ, to the unchurched, which view the float in person or through other media."

The Southern California District of the Lutheran Laymen's League has been invited to enter a float in the Rose Parade for over 55 years. The Lutheran Hour floats are sponsored by The Lutheran Hour Ministries, an auxiliary of The Lutheran Church — Missouri Synod and The Lutheran Church — Canada. For the first decade, 1950 through 1960, the float was built by volunteers from the Lutheran churches of Southern California by a group known as the Petal Pushers. Today, the Petal Pushers, a group of more than 5,000 volunteers, decorate the Lutheran Hour float as well as eight to ten additional floats., Each year, these volunteers, ranging in age from 13 to 85, travel to Pasadena from across the nation to help pay for the Lutheran Hour float through volunteer labor. They arrive after Christmas to cut flow-

The juxtaposition of this White Suiter and the 2004 Lutheran Hour Float in the background reveals, perhaps, the character of all White Suiters and Tournament of Roses volunteers.

ers and paste them, along with dried seeds, on the floats. Both young and old work into the early morning hours of New Year's Day getting the floats ready to ride down Colorado Boulevard. Individuals, church groups, families, senior citizens, and Girl Scout troops are a sample of the groups that participate each year. All float decorating volunteers must wear a Petal Pushers' Float t-shirt or sweatshirt with the current year's theme or a theme from a previous year. Many of the volunteer stay in "urban camp" on floors of local Lutheran churches. The Lutheran Hour float is the only Christian-themed float in the parade.

Once the Parade is over, the floats are parked at Post-Parade for viewing by the public for the next day and a half. Eastman Kodak reports that the Post-Parade Day is the largest single day of photographing done by individuals in the year, anywhere in the world.

FROM THE TRENCHES . . .

My first year on Post-Parade we had shut the fences after the last float, and all of us first-year people were chatting and answering the eternal questions, "How much does it cost?" and "When will it open?" Then, a fairly wizened HAM operator next to me leaned over and said, "There's another float."

I laughed along with his joke, but he shook his head and insisted, "There's another float!"

I looked at him and said, "Which float? Where?"

He answered, "Casique, and it's down at the overpass."

I looked at what seemed like two or three thousand people, already pushing up against the fence as they waited for admission, and groaned. The experienced White Suiters were many yards away, up on the curb, and didn't seem interested in the problem.

So we started talking. We waited until the float was in sight and, basically, begged all those people to let us re-open the gate and let the float in. And they did! Some did so grudgingly, others happily, and some angrily.

I think I even got a note addressed to the Tournament of Roses saying how well we had handled the situation. It certainly brought us first-year people together.

The second year on Post-Parade it rained for most of it. Two little ladies came to Paloma and Sierra Madre and said they had lost their car. It was in the handicapped parking by a school.

I started out on the scooter and went by the two elementary schools and Pasadena High School. No car.

I went back and asked if they had parked up the hill on Sierra Madre, and they assured me they had not.

Forty-five wet and cold minutes later, after double-checking all handicapped parking anywhere below Madre, I went on up the hill. There was their car, in a handicapped parking space, at Don Bonito.

I was so wet and bedraggled that the sheriffs and ladies couldn't tell it was me when I reported back.

— Volunteer

The Casablanca Fans float above in 1983 carried a real trapeze act and a live Bengal tiger. The tiger can be seen on the very front of the float with his handler. They were literally in the laps of onlookers when the float got hung up on the turn for several minutes. No one was hurt.

Left, Cinderella, her Prince, and her Fairy Godmother ride in a magical coach as part of a Disney float in 2005.

These fans below, celebrate the parade in royal style.

Above, this float from Starbucks celebrates the colorful lands where coffee comes from!

This Chinese dragon costume waits for the dancers who will bring it life in the 2005 parade. Right, Raul Rodriguez and his blue macaw Sebastion get ready for the parade in 2005.

Tournament of Roses Parade floats have come a long way since these decorated bicycles in 1900 and this large wagon float in 1895.

1900
Roy Kellogg

TOURNAMENT-OF-ROSE-1900-

HOTEL

1895

The long-view of the 2004 parade shows the line of floats down Colorado Blvd. in downtown Pasadena.

Let the Game Begin!

Top, the first Rose Bowl game between the Michigan team (in the wagon) and Stanford was such a rout that for the next 14 years chariot races were held instead of football games. Below, this air-born Michigan player dives for a down over the USC player on the ground.

Let the Game Begin!

Tournament records note that, when the Tournament of Roses was in its infancy, the New Year's afternoon games at Sportsman's Park on Los Robles included a 100-yard dash, mounted riders' tilting at rings with lances, a tug of war, and a football game between two teams of college boys, home from school for the holidays. In the next few years, bicycle races track and field events were added to what became such a long program that the pole vault had to be completed by moonlight. In 1901 polo was introduced to the agenda and held on Patton Field, an acreage at the present location of California Street and Wilson Avenue. The Tournament purchased the 14-acre site for $6,300 the following November, naming it Tournament Park (now CalTech's athletic field) and deeding it to the City of Pasadena, subsequently leasing it from the city for Tournament activities. Intersectional college football was first played in 1902, between Michigan and Stanford. Michigan beat Stanford soundly, 49-0. Net receipts for that game were recorded at $3,161.86. As the crowd of spectators arrived for the game, it soon became apparent that the 1,000 seats would not be enough. The mob of 8,500 who showed up created a stampede. No one was seriously injured, but due to the "over-excitement" of the crowd and the "lop-sided score," officials abandoned the football idea and went back to polo. Only about 2,000 people attended the games in 1903. Inspired by the recently published book, *Ben Hur*, the Tournament officials decided to introduce chariot races as part of the roster of events. Between

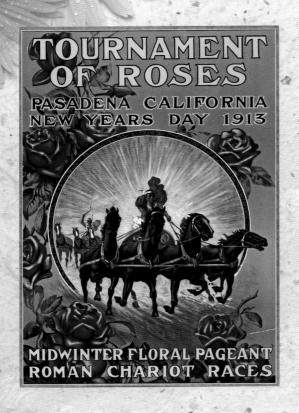

BUT, THEY'RE EXPECTING ME!

Charles Cherniss reports in the December 17, 2002 issue of the *Pasadena Star News* that "In the early '20s the Tournament of Roses hired a marathon champ to leave Tournament Park early on New Year's morning, run to the top of Mount Wilson and back, arriving to the hoped-for cheers of the football crowd at halftime. The runner did exactly as instructed, but ran into a major hitch. He didn't have a ticket to the game and the gate ushers refused to admit him."

1902 and 1916 football was dropped from the Tournament because officials couldn't get a West Coast team to play the stronger Mid-Western teams.

The 1913 event included an ostrich race, a race between an American cowboy, a cowgirl, a Mexican, and an Indian. The elephant balked near the finish line, refusing to budge. One of the ostriches threw its rider. Both a Queen and a King officiated at the Tournament that year and the next.

By 1915, the crowd of afternoon Tournament fans had increased to 25,000. The officials decided to schedule a football game between Brown and Washington State for 1916. From that year on, football became the highlight of Pasadena's New Year's afternoon.

In 1922, the Tournament built a 50,000 seat stadium in the Arroyo Seco, a picturesque dry riverbed on the northwest edge of the city of Pasadena, for at a cost of $272,298. The money was raised by Tournament of Roses volunteers. Bill Leishman's grandfather, William L. Leishman, had the idea for the Bowl's location and design. He came to Pasadena from Connecticut, home of the Yale Bowl. The stadium was named *The Rose Bowl* and dedicated in 1923, hosting its first game between USC and Penn State. USC won, 14-3. The game that pitted the legendary Four Horsemen from Notre Dame against Ernie Nevers of Stanford took place in 1925. Notre Dame won, 27-10.

In 1928 the stadium was enlarged by 19,000 seats, increasing its capacity to 76,000. The next year, Roy Riegels made the most infamous play of Rose Bowl history, running the wrong way with the ball and thus acquiring the nickname "Wrong Way Riegels."

In 1942, during World War II, the Rose Bowl game was played at Duke University in Durham, North Carolina. Once the War ended in 1946, a groundbreaking Rose Bowl Game agreement was signed between the Pacific Coast (Pac-8) and Western (Big Ten) conferences. Modified in 1960, it is the oldest college football agreement between two major conferences in the United States.

The Rose Bowl's press box was renovated in 1992, increasing its seating capacity from approximately 330 to more than 1,200.

People say that there are "no bad seats" in the Rose Bowl. The field is a crowned field, which means that the center is higher than the edges, in order to promote good drainage. It is one of the most "football-friendly" stadiums, in that there is no track around the field. The sidelines are right on the field. The steps of the stadium rise at a constant slope through Row 72. Even the highest seats allow the spectator a close view of the game. The measurement from the rim of the stadium to the edge of the field is less than that distance for any other stadium in the United States. The most popular seats, of course, are within 10 yards of the 50-yard line. After the passage of the Americans' Disability Act, the stadium's 102,000 seating capacity was reduced to 92,000 to accommodate the building of a handicapped seating area midway up, all around the rim. This area offers more

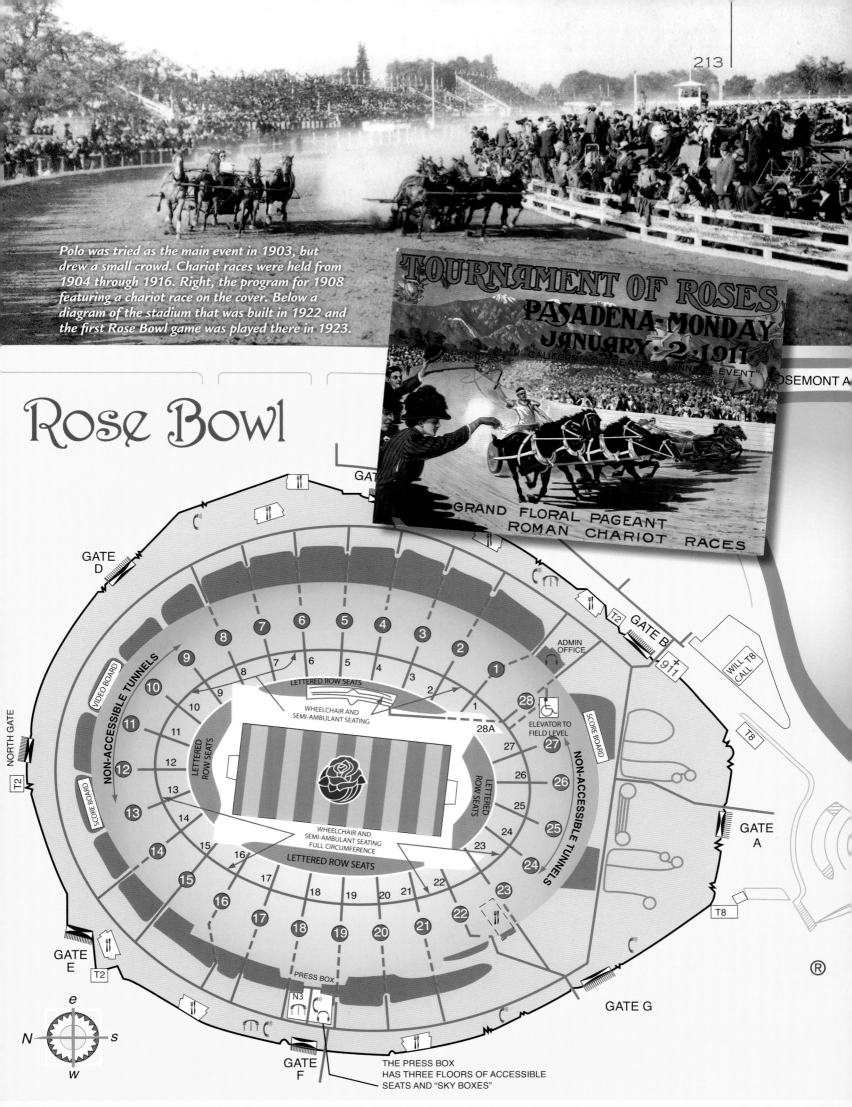

Polo was tried as the main event in 1903, but drew a small crowd. Chariot races were held from 1904 through 1916. Right, the program for 1908 featuring a chariot race on the cover. Below a diagram of the stadium that was built in 1922 and the first Rose Bowl game was played there in 1923.

TOURNAMENT OF ROSES
PASADENA·MONDAY
JANUARY·2·1911
"CALIFORNIA'S GREATEST ANNUAL EVENT"

GRAND FLORAL PAGEANT
ROMAN CHARIOT RACES

Rose Bowl

GATE D

GATE B

ROSEMONT A

WILL CALL

ADMIN OFFICE

ELEVATOR TO FIELD LEVEL

SCORE BOARD

NORTH GATE

VIDEO BOARD

NON-ACCESSIBLE TUNNELS

SCORE BOARD

NON-ACCESSIBLE TUNNELS

LETTERED ROW SEATS

WHEELCHAIR AND SEMI-AMBULANT SEATING

LETTERED ROW SEATS

LETTERED ROW SEATS

WHEELCHAIR AND SEMI-AMBULANT SEATING FULL CIRCUMFERENCE

LETTERED ROW SEATS

GATE A

GATE E

GATE G

PRESS BOX

GATE F

THE PRESS BOX HAS THREE FLOORS OF ACCESSIBLE SEATS AND "SKY BOXES"

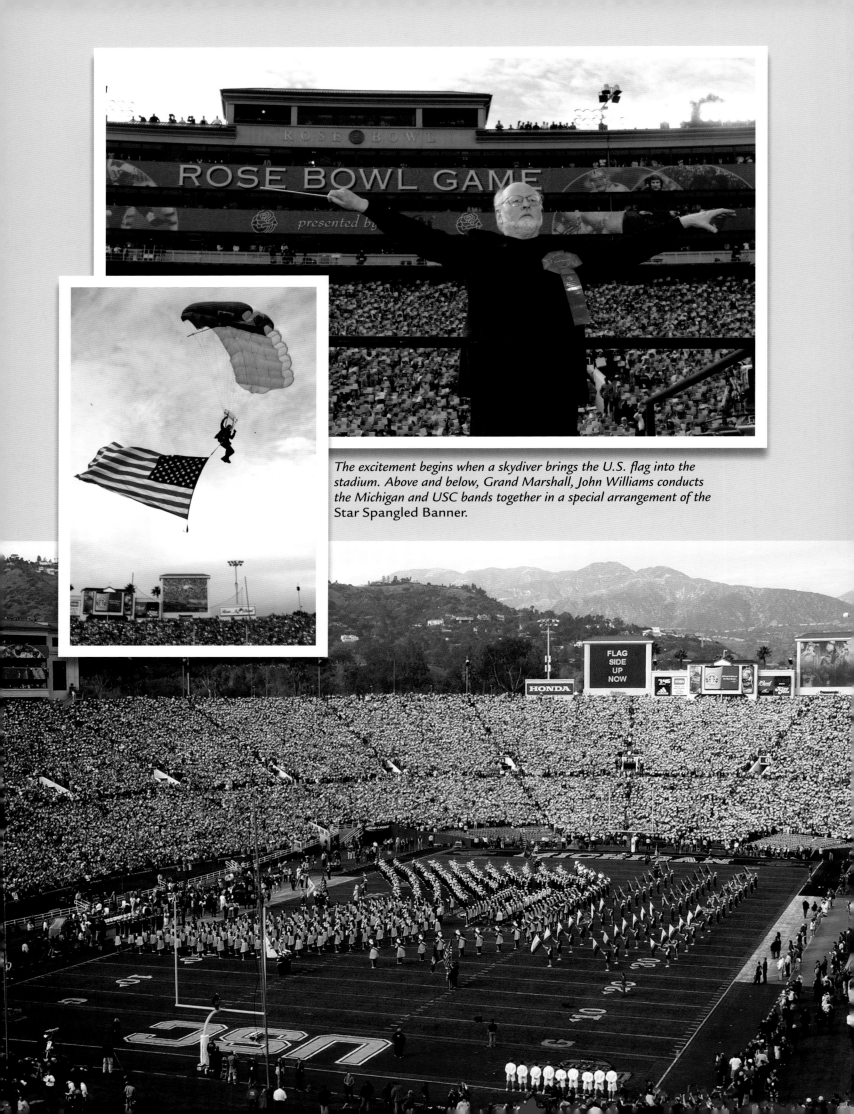

The excitement begins when a skydiver brings the U.S. flag into the stadium. Above and below, Grand Marshall, John Williams conducts the Michigan and USC bands together in a special arrangement of the Star Spangled Banner.

The opening ceremony is capped by a thrilling fly-by of a stealth bomber and two stealth fighters. Below, the audience gets in the act too, with an en mass card trick, revealing the stars and stripes on a grand scale.

THE STAR SPANGLED BANNER

Arranged especially for the Rose Bowl Ceremonies, January 1, 2004

Arranged by

J O H N W I L L I A M S

CONCERT BAND

Left, Grand Marshall John Williams tosses the coin at the start of the 2004 Rose Bowl Game. Always a heated rivalry, USC and Michigan battle out another one with USC taking the prize. These two teams have met in the Rose Bowl six times and USC has bested Michigan four times.

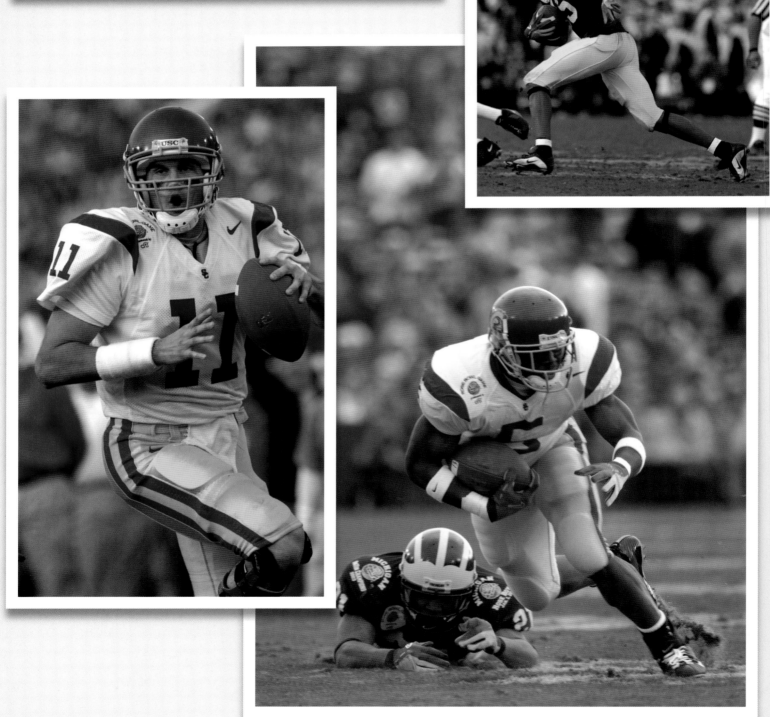

legroom for handicapped fans and their caregivers.

The Rose Bowl is UCLA's home field, per a new 20-year contract. The Bowl is restricted by the City of Pasadena to 11 events per year, including concerts, swap meets, and games.

When the opposing teams come to Pasadena for the Rose Bowl Game, they are treated like royalty. Alex

Gaal comments, "Lawry's always graciously hosted the two visiting teams and the Queen and her Court. There were players who could eat as many as eight prime ribs, plus mashed potatoes and spinach, and then ask the Princess at the table to order a second prime rib for herself so that the player could take her "second" back to his hotel in a doggy bag, still hungry!"

Another anecdote from Alex: "One year the competing teams, coaches, and the Queen and her Court

were guests for the day at Disneyland, including an elaborate dinner for about 175 people. We were all on the sky ride in those carts when a malfunction power outage stranded all carts. Disney was not prepared to rescue us, and they had to call in the Santa Ana Fire Department with their long ladders. It was cold, getting dark, and near 5:00 p.m. Seven of the Indiana players offered their jackets to the seven girls to keep them warm. Indiana Coach John Pont was upset and worried that his players were exposing themselves to the cold weather. After an hour's delay we were all rescued and proceeded to the dinner celebration. We sent Coach Pont a photo of the rescue operation."

Still another Alex story: "At

The **Bowl Championship Series** is comprised of six major college football conferences and one independent, Notre Dame, under the National College Athletic Association (NCAA) throughout the United States:

Atlantic Coast Conference
Big 10 Conference
Big 12 Conference
Big East Conference
Pac 10 Conference
Southeast Conference

Each Conference ranks its championship teams each year. The Rose Bowl has been the site for the Big 10/Pac 10 Conference playoffs since 1947.

Four Bowls host the national championship playoff games in sequential rotation: first the Fiesta Bowl, then the Sugar Bowl, next the Orange Bowl, and finally the Rose Bowl. The first national Conference playoff game was

played in 1999 at the Fiesta Bowl. The Rose Bowl's first hosting of the national championship took place in 2002, when Miami played Nebraska.

2006 was the next year that the Rose Bowl hosted the national championship game. The eight-year contract that set up the national championship sequence will expire in 2006. A new $300 million national championship contract with ABC television is a ten-game contract, good through 2014. Each Bowl will now be able to have its own traditional Conference playoff game on January 1. Eight to ten days later, one of the Bowls in normal rotation will host the national championship game. Television revenues go back to the Conferences, to the tune of $13.5 million per game. Conferences split that revenue equally among their members, which means that each school in a Conference typically gets $1 million beyond expenses.

Christmas parties hosted by the Tournament, we would present a Rose Bowl wristwatch to each player and coach. This was the main gift. One player approached me after the presentation and insisted that his box did not contain a watch. I explained that 60 boxes were put on a table and checked three times by three different members before the gifts were wrapped. He sheepishly walked away.

"Several months after a game I received a call from a local school player saying his apartment had been burglarized and his Rose Bowl watch had been stolen. I asked him for a copy of the LAPD report on the incident. He said he would get back to me. I never heard from him again."

I enjoy learning Tournament history from the people who made it happen. Don Anderson graciously allowed me to view his three beautiful and irreplaceable albums that commemorate his family's involvement in the Tournament. Don's family business has been a customer of Citizens' Business Bank since 1912. His father was a bank customer before him. He was also President of the Tournament of Roses in 1935 and 1936. The albums contain articles and pictures that tell the dismal story of the 1934 rains that threatened to shut the Parade down. It rained so hard that year that the Rose Bowl was flooded. Ironically, that year was the first time the Parade's theme

PAC-10 Conference:
Arizona State University
Oregon State University
Stanford University
University of Arizona
University of California, Berkeley
University of California, Los Angeles
University of Oregon
University of Southern California
University of Washington
Washington State University

Big 10 Conference:
Michigan State University
Northwestern University
Ohio State University
Penn State University
Purdue
University of Illinois
University of Indiana
University of Iowa
University of Michigan
University of Minnesota
University of Wisconsin

2004 University of Michigan float. U of M is in the Big 10 Conference and has made 16 appearances in the Rose Bowl (as of 2006). Michigan played in the first game in 1902, and shut out Stanford, 49-0.

Opposite page, the 2004 float for University of Southern California of the PAC 10. USC has appeared 29 times, more than any other team, and has a 21-8 record at the Rose Bowl (as of 2006).

had to do with water: "Tale of the Seven Seas." No Parade has used a water-related theme since.

Stan Hahn, Member Emeritus, joined the Tournament in 1937. "There were no women involved with the Tournament then," he notes, "but there weren't any women on the Supreme Court then, either." Hahn had attended his first Tournament football game at age 10, in 1920, at Tournament Park before the Rose Bowl was finished. He was in the crowd in 1923 when the first game at the Bowl was played. He graduated from Pasadena High School in 1927, moving on to Pomona College. His father was appointed to judgeship in 1920. Stan was sent to Harvard Law School during the Great Depression, and remembers that era well. He returned and passed the California Bar Exam, beginning his law practice in 1934.

Pasadena was still a small town, and his was a "one-car family" with two children. He joined the Tournament "in order to meet other nice people" and because his law firm, which had been founded by his father and uncle in 1899, advised its partners to "do one thing for the outside community, and do it right."

"The Bowl didn't sell all that well back then," Hahn remarks, "except for the 1925 Pop Warner/Knute Rockne game when the Four Horsemen played. PAC 10 lost the first 10 or 11 games."

The college presidents had reservations about our motives. Back then, they sent faculty reps to our meetings at Cal Tech. Now, the presidents come themselves and there is a great deal of academic interest in the prestige gained by playing in the Rose Bowl."

During World War II, the game had to be moved to Duke University, back East. The armed forces needed to keep the Pacific

Stan Hahn, shown with Lay Leishman and Paul Bryant in 1962.

Coast Highway cleared of crowds. No headlights were allowed on that highway at night during the war, as they could be seen clearly from the sea.

Hahn notes that the networks were reluctant to buy in during the 1950s. He played golf with John West, the "head NBC man on the West Coast." NBC offered to pay $250,000 to cover

the Tournament. "We weren't such a plum back then, from an advertising viewpoint." Later, Hahn was to take over as chair of the Football Committee during the switchover from NBC to ABC. This time, the offer was $5 million. Bob Iger was the head of ABC, and came to the Tournament House to meet with Stan and other committee members. "He was great to deal with," notes Stan. "He was fair, and he understood our problems." Ray Dorn had been instrumental in Pasadena's acquiring the Tournament House from the Wrigley family. "I carried his briefcase," Hahn quips, although he participated in arranging the city's lease of the house to the Tournament for $1.00 per year.

Hahn has witnessed major changes since 1937. The Tournament has become "Big Business," subject to tax laws and government control. But "the commitment to integrity is still the same," he asserts, even though the size of the membership is greater. He recalls great friends like Wayne Duke and Don Cannon. "We tried to keep it so that the PAC 10 teams would only 'do' the Rose Bowl," he says. "But they were getting offers to do other bowls, and they needed to make money. Leishman got a suitcase and took it to a meeting, labeling it 'Pandora's Box.' 'This is what will happen if we allow teams to play in other bowls,' he said, opening the box and letting all kinds of things fly out. But we had to give in."

When we asked him to tell us an "in between the lines" story, Stan was reminded of the 1955 Tournament, when Elmer Wilson was president. This was Stan's first close encounter with security issues.

Wilson's Grand Marshal was Chief Justice Earl Warren. My cousin, Herbert Hahn, was a close friend of his at Stanford. I was in charge of the Brookside luncheon that year. It rained, and we had to move the luncheon inside. In the middle of it all the Chief of Police Stan Decker called to tell me that a crank call had been received. Stan came over with five or six men who stood near the head table, facing the crowd. Mrs. Warren and Lou Edwards arrived. "Do we tell the Chief Justice?" I asked.

"Not now," was the reply.

Nothing happened. Those six guys rode to the game in a car right behind the Chief Justice when it was time to go to the game. Nothing ever happened.

USC fans cheer on their team and predict the outcome of the game in 2004.

2005 brought a newly-designed championship trophy to the Rose Bowl game. Designed by Tiffany & Co. in cooperation with the Tournament, it features a sterling silver football set upon a multi-tiered platform on sterling silver rods. Its official name is The Leishman Trophy, in honor of 1920 Tournament of Roses President William L. Leishman, who was responsible for the construction of the Rose Bowl Stadium, and his son, 1939 Tournament of Roses President Lathrop K. Leishman. I think that the new trophy is really gorgeous. The previous trophy was first used at the 1989 Rose Bowl Game, and it was so heavy that I

Head Coach, Pete Carroll of USC hoists the Leishman Trophy overhead after the team's successful 2004 game.

Opposite, the Michigan band plays with gusto during their halftime routine. Inset, members of the U of M pep squad are well known for their acrobatic stunts.

Above, the USC pepsquad bounds onto the field ahead of their team. Left, Traveller, the USC Trojan horse mascot is a crowd favorite and celebrates each USC touchdown with a sprint down the sideline. Below the USC band "gets down."

Mike and Anne Riffey, Grand Marshal John Williams, the Royal Court, and others receive last minute instructions before heading out to the field before the game.

The USC Band Director smiles as he strides down the sideline before his band's performance.

The Michigan receiver spots the pass as he runs downfield...

The catch looks good...

The University of Michigan drill team bounds on to the field with enthusiasm.

Seriously Focused Michigan Wolverine officials.

Skydivers parachute over the stadium with colored smoke.

Wait! Has he got the ball?

No.

CHAPTER 11

You're On the Air!

A crane holds media cameras over the street to capture the action in the 1960s. This arrangement would be too low for the high-rise floats of today.

You're On the Air!

By 1930, the Rose Parade was being broadcast in word pictures by radio all over the world. Motion pictures and newsreels were shown in theaters. In the United States today, the Rose Parade is seen on ABC, CBS, NBC, the Travel Channel, Discovery HD Theater, KMEX-TV, HGTV, KTLA, and Telemundo. In addition it is broadcast in more than 50 countries.

Ronald Reagan was extensively involved with coverage for the Tournament of Roses. He covered the Parade for ABC from the late 1950s through 1961, and then moved to CBS to cover the event until 1966. As Governor of California, Reagan attended many Rose Bowl Games. In 1987, during his second term as President of the United States, he signed legislation making the rose America's national flower.

Stephanie Edwards has been working with Bob Eubanks as a KTLA television commentator for the Rose Parade for about 27 years. Bob held the position with other hosts for a few years before Stephanie joined him. At the time she took the Tournament job, she was hosting a morning show in Los Angeles and was the spokesperson for Lucky Supermarkets. "I really did a good job," she quips, "Lucky's is no longer in business." She and her husband, Murray MacLeod, have not celebrated New Year's Eve most of that time, which suits them fine because they are not "partiers." I can relate. When the Parade is held until January 2nd every seventh year, Anne and I don't really know what to do on New Year's Eve — we're too used to having Tournament work to do.

Stephanie recalls her first Tournament broadcast as if it were yesterday: she says that she was "scared to death," and Bob tried to calm her down by joking with her. She's a refreshing character, born and raised in the farm country of Minnesota. Educated at St. Olaf College, she moved to Los Angeles after graduation seeking a career in broadcasting. She worked with Ralph Story, to whom she refers as "my beloved mentor," on a morning show that became the prototype for *Good Morning, America*. She is the national spokesperson for a charity that is raising money to house and educate children in Kenya who have been orphaned by the AIDS epidemic. She worries that American children are being raised to "see and want," rather than "think and do," and she tries to show young people everywhere that they will have a variety of assignments and adventures during their lifetimes, all of which will be "real" work.

Stephanie and Bob's New Year's work actually begins well before the Parade. One or two days after Christmas, Stephanie, Bob, and several other KTLA staff members go to the float barns. They examine each float, meet the builders and designers, and chat with the volunteers to help prepare for the broadcast. "The drivers are a ribald, hilarious, irreverent, courageous bunch. Some of them are women." She reminisces fondly about how their early producer, director, writer, the late Bill Rainbolt, would accompany them. Bill was

hired each year by KTLA to do the Parade broadcast. "Bill was one of a kind, and he was ecstatic about Parades. He had to know, and wanted us to know, every bolt and blossom on every float, even though there was no chance of our getting every detail in during the broadcast. He would climb under and over the floats to see how the animation worked, which slowed the whole entourage down. Than we would spend another two days in a closed, windowless room while Bill smoked one cigarette after another while we all mused over how to construct the script.

> "The drivers are a ribald, hilarious, irreverent, courageous bunch. Some of them are women."
> —Stephanie Edwards

He insisted on our driving out to, say, Pomona (where half of the Cal Poly float is constructed each year) to shoot the promo spots that Channel 5 airs during the days between Thanksgiving and New Year's. He wanted to be sure to portray the float atmosphere 'on location' . . . usually in the early morning in a cold, driving wind. The joke of it was that we'd end up shooting the spots in front of a wall, which could have been anywhere! We laughed with him and at him during our years together. He was one of that breed who live for the Pa-

rade, and who was excited as a schoolboy each year. We remember him very fondly. By the same token, however, we are glad that the preparation process has been streamlined considerably since those days."

On New Year's Eve, Stephanie usually heads for bed at around 8:00 p.m. She gets up on New Year's Day early enough to drive to KTLA by 4:30 a.m. She comments that she can provide living proof for global warming: 27 years ago she would wear long underwear, layer on layer of clothing, gloves, hats, and scarves. Now, she usually sheds her jacket by mid-Parade because the weather is warmer. (Anne and I still recommend layered clothing to all Parade viewers, however: if you plan to spend the night or get to a grandstand early enough in the morning to avoid traffic complications, it is wise to bring a blanket to sit on, gloves, and a hat or scarf.)

From the studio, Stephanie and Bob are driven by limousine to the Parade broadcast location. She mentions that, since September 11, 2001, it has taken longer for the limo to navigate the security checkpoints. On New Year's Day 2005, Bob had to get out of the car three or four times to identify himself and Stephanie, and they were worried that they might not make it to their location on time.

Once they are dropped off at the KTLA trailer on location, it is time for makeup. Bob's takes about 10 minutes; Stephanie's takes about 50 minutes. "Even

EXCERPTS FROM THE KTLA SCRIPT FOR 2005

Bob: This is the American Honda float, FAMILIES ACROSS AMERICA, and at 207 feet long, the longest ever in a Rose Parade, it just about does stretch across America.

The steam-spewing engine is being driven by Phoenix Floats' "Engineer Bill" Lofthouse. It's been decorated with red carnation petals, ground sweet rice and blue statice, and so has the tender car.

Stephanie: Next in line is the celebration car, which features real pyrotechnics. In fact, a special permit was required by the Pasadena Fire Department in order to set them off.

Last but not least, the family car, carrying members of the Honda family, is covered with orange and yellow strawflowers with silverleaf trim.

Bob: This year marks the beginning of Phoenix Floats' Bill Lofthouse's 50th year in the business. It also marks the first time he's ever actually participated in the Parade.

Stephanie: Honda has won major Rose Parade awards in nine of the last ten years for their floats.

. . .

Bob: This year, the City of Torrance observes its 51st appearance in the Rose Parade, which is definitely SOMETHING TO CROW ABOUT.

A county fair provides the backdrop for bees buzzing around huge sunflowers, a feast of good food and a good old-fashioned square-dance, with a 14-foot-tall crow calling out the steps.

Stephanie: And the chicks just love him. However, in this case, they're freshly-hatched babies covered with strawflowers.

The calling crow's feathering is created with black lichen moss and his outfit is a combination of red, orange, and yellow strawflowers, with lavender spice overalls.

The beautiful sunflowers found throughout this float are fashioned with yellow strawflowers with hot orange Mercedes roses in the middle.

Bob: This float is decorated by volunteers from the City of Torrance, aged 13 to well over 80.

. . .

Bob: The Painted Ladies Rodeo Performers, led by their Marshal Jennifer Macias Sweeny, have been together for more than ten years and are all riding their beautiful paint horses. The difference between a Paint horse and a Pinto horse is that a paint horse is a breed and has strict bloodline requirements, whereas a pinto is a color and can be found in many breeds. This group is a mounted drill team that performs all over, showing off their incredible riding skills and their paint horses.

. . .

Bob: Here's another band making their Rose Parade debut. Welcome to the Pasadena Unified School District All-Star Band.

Optional: This band was assembled specifically to appear in the Rose Parade. Members of this band come from Blair, John Muir, John Marshall Fundamental, and Pasadena High Schools and the Elliot, McKinley, Norma Coombs Alternative, Sierra Madre, Washington, and Wilson Middle Schools. Karrie Willett is this new organization's executive director. 1977 was the last time a band from the Pasadena Unified School District appeared in the Rose Parade. It was the Pasadena High Band.

Bob: Our thanks to the brand spanking new Pasadena Unified School District All-Star Band for starting out the new year with us.

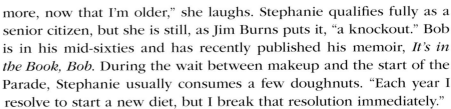

more, now that I'm older," she laughs. Stephanie qualifies fully as a senior citizen, but she is still, as Jim Burns puts it, "a knockout." Bob is in his mid-sixties and has recently published his memoir, *It's in the Book, Bob*. During the wait between makeup and the start of the Parade, Stephanie usually consumes a few doughnuts. "Each year I resolve to start a new diet, but I break that resolution immediately."

Actually, the camera doesn't focus in on Stephanie or Bob all that often, as KTLA's emphasis is on the Parade entries, not the commentators. KTLA broadcasts from a booth located high over the Parade route, across the street from the Norton Simon Museum at the corner of Colorado Boulevard and Orange Grove. A "cherry picker" truck hoists them to the booth, as Bob hates heights and the steps to the booth are many and steep. The booth has its own "Porta Potty," which is of course small and uncomfortable to use, especially in the morning when it is dark. One year, Stephanie's digestive system was extremely upset, and she had misgivings about having such limited facilities available for the duration of the Parade. Her makeup artist hurried across the parking lot to the Elk's Club to get some boiled milk for her, and that solved the problem. There have been a couple of years when Bob had really bad colds, but he managed to get through the Parades successfully. The commentators' script is about five inches thick; it is given to them days in advance. The research and writing is done by Ira Lawson, hired especially for this event, and longtime Executive Producer Joe Quasarano. Stickers have been placed on the appropriate pages at the very last minute, labeling the floats that have won awards. Stephanie and Bob review the script well ahead of time, deciding which of them will talk about each Parade entry. Bob is an expert on horses and their riders' outfits, since he is an equestrian himself; she has a soft spot for bands, as she was a trombone player in high school and marched in the band. Trombones usually march in the front of the band, and the first trombone player sets the pace.

During the broadcast they wear large earphones because the ambient noise of the Parade can be distracting. Their Emmy-winning director, Stephanie Medina, communicates with them through the earphones, prompting them each time a new float rounds the corner and shushing them when it's time to let the audience hear a band or a loudspeaker. Stephanie Edwards is fascinated by the details of each float's design and construction, and wants to share all of them with the audience. She chuckles as she describes how Bob puts his hand on her wrist when she talks too long about a float. If she keeps talking, his grip gets tighter and tighter. She and Bob enjoy their spirited banter during the broadcast. They sometimes get letters (not a lot of

Parade fans smile for the camera.

Above, an NBC cameraman films the Parade in 1987. Below, this newspaper ad from the 1940s advises that you can install your TV in as little as 5 minutes and urges you to purchase one to watch the Parade and game.

The media set up their equipment on the high stands in preparation for the Parade in 1971. Below, production personnel in a broadcast control room, mixes shots of the Parade for live viewing by the world-wide audience in 1987. The Tournament of Roses Parade is one of the most watched TV broadcasts in the world.

The production booth overlooking the Rose Bowl Game in 2004.

them) asking why they dislike each other, and the station management has asked them to play down their repartee, which Bob and Stephanie at first feared would diminish their own enjoyment of the assignment. During the most recent Parade broadcast, however, they did as they had been asked and felt that their rapport was actually extra-good. Stephanie grudgingly admits, smiling, that management "may have been right, after all. We wouldn't joke about each other on the air if we really did dislike each other," she says, "but some viewers evidently thought our little jabs at each other's expense were less affectionate than we felt. So we had to pull in a bit." They often have much more information to share about floats, bands, and equestrian units than they have time for. The Parade moves along at a pretty good pace, which minimizes on camera time. Even though they do not wish for a float to break down, when they do or there are other delays in the Parade's progress, it gives them time to refer to their notes to share more information. They are careful not to broadcast any problems that occur during the Parade, such as demonstrations or injuries to people or horses. Stephanie feels that the Rose Queens are more polished and mature these days than they were when she first began working with the Parade.

After one Parade, Stephanie was introduced to Angie Dickinson and her daughter, who were sitting right below the broadcast booth. Angie thanked Stephanie for the use, over many years, of the restroom located in Stephanie's dressing trailer behind the grandstand. Stephanie was surprised and thrilled that Angie had been using her facilities, and told her, "I'm going to put this on my resume!"

After the Parade is over, the stands and streets fill immediately with exiting spectators. Gypsy Boots, a long time L.A. area character was a part of that entourage until his passing in 2004. Stephanie and Bob are lowered by the cherry picker and make their way to the waiting limousine, which inches slowly through the traffic back to their KTLA station in Hollywood. Both ride silently for awhile, and then begin to critique the performance. Back at the station, Stephanie gets into her own car and heads for home, turning on the radio to listen to music. She says she always remembers the "first song of the new year." The magnitude of the contrast between the huge crowds that surrounded her at the Parade and her post-Parade solitude always affects her profoundly,

Once she gets home, she takes a nap while her visiting family watches the game on television. Says she, "I get more TLC than I deserve that day. After all, they've been up almost as long as I have, carrying blankets and walking and waiting in the cold."

News affiliates, networks and broadcasters from all over the world report live from the Parade and game every year. Jann Carl anchors the CBS Parade broadcast booth in 2005.

Below, reporters scramble to file their stories during, and after the Rose Bowl Game in 2004.

Reporters stand on the multi-tiered media stands, observing and taking pictures at the 1989 Parade. Below, security at the Rose Bowl Game in 2004 uses the same control booth area as game media to keep an eye on the crowds.

Main photo, the media stands are still in use today and offer a good vantage point for this security officer. Above, in 1967 this Pasadena police officer uses the live media broadcast to monitor the Parade crowds in the command center.

CHAPTER 12

Aftermaths, Memories, and Futures

People streaming past the floats in the Sierra Madre post-parade viewing area.

Aftermaths, Memories, and Future

When the Parade and the Game are all over, and the post-game partiers have gone home, quiet descends on the Pasadena streets. Crews work late into the night, taking down scaffolding and lights and restoring the thoroughfares in preparation for the morning traffic. Tons of trash are collected by the City of Pasadena's refuse collectors. The floats sit silently, in their last moments of grandeur and perfume, waiting for the last viewers to leave so that they can be taken back to the float barns and disassembled. The band kids fall sleep gratefully in hotel rooms or on planes and buses, dreaming of scenes from their long march. The horses are ready for the comfort of their familiar home stables.

The Tournament members will spend about three weeks debriefing and wrapping up their records and ledgers. Then, toward the end of January, the Float Entries Chairperson will be in charge of the annual Tournament Retreat at Rancho Santa Fe. This is where the Tournament Chairpersons, Directors, and the Executive Committee will do a final critique of the year's events and turn their minds toward the future once again. The retreat begins on Friday afternoon with golf and a barbecue at Rancho Santa Fe. Saturday's highlight is a guest speaker and a luncheon.

Gary DiSano was in charge of the Rancho excursion after the 2001 parade. Here is is account, which he titles as "A Recounting of the Mt. Palomar Excursion":

It all started with the Tournament of Roses Float Entries Committee's working on the Rancho Excursion, traditionally

Tons O' Tuba

When I felt as if the weight of my tuba was 1,000 pounds and I was going to give up at any moment, the people shouting at us "You can make it!" is what kept me going. Even though they were complete strangers, they knew how we felt and what we were thinking. That is what sticks out most of the entire parade: the people. All of them. The people watching, the people encouraging, the people giving out water, the people taking care of the sick, all of them. They'll never know that it was because of them that I was able to march for five and a half miles with a tuba, to complete a parade that I shall never forget.

—Jessica Simpson, Age 18

an opportunity for bonding and time together within the hierarchy and leadership of the Tournament. We wanted to do something different. We had done many military outings lately, so the Committee decided to try dining under the 200-inch telescope on Mt. Palomar, which we were told was a rare occurrence. The field trip/busing/catering was all in place. We were told that the telescope mirror might fog up, but that minor snowfall at the time of year when we were planning to go was a rarity.

When the Rancho weekend came, rain had passed through and a few broken clouds dotted the sky. All looked well. The buses were loaded. We asked the drivers if they had chains, just in case they might be needed, and were told, "No problem! We got 'em."

The drive started. As we approached the 3,000 foot level, we noticed snow on the road. The buses chugged through without much problem — a little slip here and a little slide there — a little heart thrill now and then, but no biggie . . . yet.

Then it began to snow a bit more heavily. The bus drivers and their passengers grew quiet. "Have you ever driven in snow before?" someone queried. Unfortunately, one of the drivers had had only a little experience with snow, and the other driver had had none. We were about a half-mile from the top of the mountain when the Highway Patrol pulled up and stopped us to explain that we would not be allowed to continue without chains.

Everyone got out of the buses and stood in the snow. A few tossed snowballs at each other. Meanwhile, the "Risk Management (ad hoc) Committee," led by Mike Riffey, met to discuss the situation. As is always the case with the Tournament, the committee decided that safety wins out, even over eating lunch that is prepared and waiting under a famous telescope at the top of a mountain.

The caterer ate the luncheon with the Mt. Palomar crew and the Float Entries Committee Members. The 100 or so Chairpersons and Directors and Executive Committee members headed back down the mountain, still slipping and sliding and hanging on for dear life.

Everyone did get a Mt. Palomar cap with the Tournament of Roses logo on it, along with a good story to tell. Mike Riffey okayed the expense of a quickly-arranged lunch at the base of the mountain. The Float Entries Chair received an apology and a refund from the bus company.

Gary's disappointment was absolutely understandable, and I felt bad to have to turn those buses back. It is always hard to be the Tournament official who is faced with denying a new idea or turning down a plan or giving a demerit to a non-compliant float. But lives are precious and irreplacable, and the Tournament has always valued

People come out to see, photograph, and even sniff their favorite bit of Tournament of Roses history.

Parade goers leave a mess in their wake in 1970. A few hours later, a lone street sweeper removes the last evidence of a perfect Rose Parade.

safety over risk. Everything focused around New Year's Day should be about beginnings, and it should be as free of worry or pain as possible.

I will always remember my Tournament heroes: Brian Paciulan, Jason Cole, Fred Rogers; unknown heroes like the Big Bear Eagle Scout with multiple sclerosis, who carried the 1986 President's banner in his wheelchair, and so many others who have given every ounce of energy to make the world more beautiful. Each story that has been shared with you here can be matched by thousands of others — no single book could hold them all. But they have, I hope, given you a glimpse behind the scenes and shown you a bit of the Tournament's complexity and spirit.

People dedicate their lives to the Tournament; it's more than a labor of love — it's giving time, financial sacrifice, and separation from one's own family on an annual basis. People open up to each other on that day; everyone likes everybody; everyone is your friend. It is delightful to see a White Suiter approach an older couple on Parade day, as they ponder the immensity of the grandstand and wonder how to find their seats. They're amazed when the "official" offers to walk them to their seats, instead of just pointing them in the right direction. That's the spirit of service and attention to individual needs that the Tournament Association is all about. It really is much more than a Parade.

I hope that each person who reads this book will be moved to tell his or her own New Year's Day story. They're all important, and they're all worth sharing.

For me, New Year's Day 2004 was the most perfect day in the world. Yes, exhaustion hit about a week after it was all over, but that was nothing in comparison with the joy, pride, and sense of community that I feel because I am part of the Tournament of Roses family.

Again, Happy New Year to you, always!

MY FIVE SECONDS

It was the day after we had returned from California. I was lounging on the sofa, reading *Gone with the Wind* and waiting for the dryer to finish drying my three band shirts and parade jacket. Scarlett was about to marry her sister's sweetheart when the phone rang. It was my grandmother.

"Christy? How are you doing?"

"All right," I replied.

"Well, I just wanted to let you know that I watched you on TV. I was watching HGTV and I saw your school, but I didn't see you at first," Grandma continued as her voice began to become more unsteady. "Then I flipped to the Travel Channel, and there you were. They showed a picture of you for almost five seconds!"

At this she completely lost it. The sound of her broken sobs carried from Alabama to the phone at my ear. "I'm just so proud of you, my little girl! Just so proud! My little granddaughter, in the Rose Parade! I just called to let you know how proud I am of you, and how much I love you."

The Rose Parade was an awesome experience, but the most awesome thing of all was that I grew closer to my grandmother, who loves me.

—Christy Weeks, Age 16

Afterword

Near the end of Mike Riffey's Tournament of Roses presidency, I visited with him in his office at Citizens Business Bank in Pasadena, California to ask him to speak in a radio advertising spot. I wanted to feature Mike relating his duties as President of the Pasadena Tournament of Roses to his work as Senior Vice President of the bank.

As I looked around his office at the many mementos and pictures, it was easy to change the subject from the radio spot to Mike's involvement with the Tournament. For two and a half hours that afternoon, I was mesmerized by story after story about Mike's experiences throughout thirty-plus years of dedicated service to this organization.

Mike's deep voice and touching words stirred a wide range of emotion in me; he shared the trials and triumphs of young band members and their directors, Rose Queens and their parents, floats and their makers, and the 900-plus folks who buy white suits and put on much more than a parade each year, for the rest of the world to enjoy.

As I discreetly wiped away accumulated drops near the corners of my eyes after one of Mike's more poignant stories, he sat back in his chair and said, "One day I will have to write a book about all of this."

My presence in Mike's office was as president of Uber Advertising & Public Relations, the agency that planned and implemented the bank's advertising campaigns. But I was also affiliated with Stephens Press. Stephens produces high quality books of regional interest.

Jim Burns (at left in green raincoat), Beth, Todd and Smith Pallett enjoy a wet parade with a damp, but loyal crowd, January 2nd, 2006.

At that moment this book was conceived.

Since then, I've interviewed Art Linkletter, Shirley Temple, Stan Chambers, Stephanie Edwards, float builders, band members and directors, and many Tournament of Roses staff members both past and present. All related story after story with me about the magic that is created on New Year's Day and shared with the world. In my mind, our purpose in creating this book was to pay tribute to all kinds of artists who care not only about an annual first-class production, but also about people.

Many years ago, a radio program invited listeners to share with the audience what they believed. It was broadcast in the '50s, and it presented topics such as trust, love, relationships, country, truth, and honor. Today, National Public Radio (NPR) is trying to revive that program by inviting listeners to submit comments about what they believe.

If I were being interviewed today for NPR's program, *I Believe*, I would say that the world is moving and changing so fast that it is not only difficult to keep up, it is difficult to connect with anyone on a personal level. Folks rush from here to there with little concern for those around them, running stop lights, cutting other motorists off in traffic, avoiding eye contact with strangers, and generally not caring about anyone unless that someone will help them get a promotion or buy something from them.

Most organizations today are becoming larger and showing less compassion for the individual.

Mike and Anne Riffey and the Pasadena Tournament of Roses don't fit that model. From the moment I met Mike and Anne, I was taken by their warmth and charm. You might immediately wonder why Mike, Senior Vice President of Citizens Business Bank and the President of the 2004 Tournament of Roses would take the time to get to know a stranger. As Mike and Anne and the many folks who run the Tournament of Roses share their stories about the spirit and passion behind the world-famous Parade and its celebrated football game, however, it will become obvious that these are people who truly care about not only the success of the events, but also the people and animals who help the world celebrate the dawn of each New Year.

To my listening audience at National Public Radio, I would state that I believe that there are people and organizations that exist to make this world we live in a bit nicer and more pleasant. I was lucky enough to meet them, and I also believe that you will find this book full of the joy of giving by which these folks and this organization live.

It has been my honor to be a part of the creation of this book, and more importantly, to find two new friends whom I will forever cherish.

—Jim Burns

Appendix

The official grandstand seating company for the Tournament of Roses is the Sharp Seating Company. Orders for seating are available by mail, by telephone, or online. Contact information is listed below. The company also handles admission to viewers to Float Decorating, Bandfest, Post-Parade, the Museum, and the Equestrian event.

Sharp Seating Company
P. O. Box 68
Pasadena, CA 91102-0068
(626) 795-4171
www.sharpseating.com

Address of the Rose Bowl Stadium: 1001 Rose Bowl Drive, Pasadena
Parking gates open at 6:00 a.m.
Stadium gates open at noon.
Pre-game activities begin at 1:30 p.m.
Kick-off is at 2:00 p.m.
Shuttle pick-up is at the corner of Union Street and Pasadena Avenue in Old Pasadena.
Park in lots throughout Old Pasadena for fees from $5 to $25.
Fanfest at Expo Village
December 28-31

Chili Cook-Off
December 30

Rose Bowl Stadium,
1001 Rose Bowl Drive, Pasadena
Admission is free.

Financial contributions (tax-deductible) can be mailed to the
Tournament of Roses Foundation
P. O. Box 91184
Pasadena, CA 91184

Float Decorating and Viewing
Rose Palace
835 South Raymond Avenue, Pasadena
Rosemont Pavilion
700 Seco Street, Pasadena

Brookside Pavilion
South Side of Rose Bowl Stadium

Buena Vist Pavilion
22144 Buena Vista, Duarte

Tournament of Roses Bandfest
Pasadena City College
1570 E. Colorado Boulevard, Pasadena
Admission $10; $5 for children 4-12; free for children 3 and under

Equestfest
Los Angeles Equestrian Center, 480 Riverside Drive, Burbank
To purchase tickets in advance, call (626) 795-4171

Rose Bowl Game Kickoff Luncheon
Rose Bowl Area L, 1001 Rose Bowl Drive, $60.00 Tickets can be purchased through Ticket-Master, (213) 480-3232

Post-Parade Float Viewing
Washington Boulevard and Sierra Madre Boulevard $7; children under 3 free $2 roundtrip shuttle from 6:45 a.m. to 5:45 p.m.

Shuttle Pickup Locations:
Pasadena City College, 1570 E. Colorado Blvd.
Community Education Center, 3035 E. Foothill Blvd.
Danone Building, 3280 Foothill Blvd.
Rose Bowl Stadium, 1001 Rose Bowl Drive

Pasadena Visitor Center
171 S. Los Robles Avenue
www.pasadenacal.com

Holiday Hotline
(877) 793-9911

Photo Credits

No book of this magnitude would be possible without the generous contribution of photos, illustrations and memorabilia from many people and organizations. The author extends sincere gratitude to the following for their assistance in providing images for the pages indicated.

Anne Riffey
Pages 52, 93, 252

Bill Uber
Page 42 (top)

California Highway Patrol
Pages 208-209

Carolyn Hayes Uber
Pages 67, 72, 73, 180, 181, 186, 187

Chris Wheeler
Pages 14, 43 (top), 76-77, 105 (top), 118-119, 122, 125, 169 (top, middle, bottom left), 172, 175 (top two), 189, 197, 204 (bottom left), 205 (bottom left), 207

David Balfour
Pages 31, 38, 48, 50, 228 (top left)

Donna Soldwedel
Page 32

Jim Burns
Pages 49, 50 (top left and bottom), 51, 175 (bottom two), 190 (bottom two)

Jim Moore
Page 170

Kathy Matsumoto
149 (middle right)

Kodak/Antonio Perez and Richard Maxson
Pages 39, 56, 100-101, 102, 108, 132-133, 162-163, 176-177, 185, 198-199

KTLA
Pages 232, 235, 239 (top)

Los Angeles Times
Page 149 (middle left)

Mikimoto America
Page 160

Pasadena Museum of History
Pages 2-3, 16 (top), 90, 151 (top eight), 153-154, 157 (top right), 192, 206 (top), 209 (top), 238 (bottom)

Pasadena Police Department
Pages 34-35, 44-45, 57, 58, 230-231

Pasadena Star-News
Page 157 (bottom left)

Pasadena Tournament of Roses
Pages 4, 6, 7, 8, 9, 10,11, 12-13, 16 (bottom), 17, 18, 19, 20, 21, 22-23, 24, 26, 27, 28, 36, 37, 38-39, 42 (bottom, left and right), 43 (bottom), 46, 53, 54-55, 56, 60-61, 65, 69, 70, 74, 75, 78, 80, 81, 83, 84, 85, 86, 87, 91, 92, 94, 96, 98, 99, 104, 105 (bottom), 107, 110, 111, 112, 114, 115, 116, 117, 119 (insets), 120-121, 127, 128 129, 131, 134, 135, 136, 137, 138, 139, 140, 141, 142-143, 144, 146, 147 (top and bottom), 150, 151 (bottom two), 152, 156, 157 (top left, bottom right), 161, 164, 166, 167 (bottom right), 171, 174, 178, 179, 182-183, 184, 190 (top two), 193, 194, 195, 204 (201, 202, 203, 204 (top, bottom right), 205 (top, bottom right), 206 (bottom), 209 (background), 215, 216, 217, 218, 221, 222, 223, 224, 225, 226, 227, 228 (top right, bottom left and right), 229, 236, 237, 238 (top), 239 (bottom), 240, 241, 242, 243, 244-245, 246, 247 248, 249, 250, 251, 252

Raul Rodriquez
Page 165

Tadashi
Pages 158-159